# lonely planet

# HONG KONG

| CONDENSED |

KT-415-618

Patrick Witton    Dani Valent

LONELY PLANET PUBLICATIONS
Melbourne • Oakland • London • Paris

# contents

Hong Kong Condensed
2nd edition – March 2003
First published – January 2001

Published by
Lonely Planet Publications Pty Ltd
ABN 36 005 607 983
90 Maribyrnong St, Footscray, Vic 3011, Australia
e www.lonelyplanet.com or AOL keyword: lp

Lonely Planet offices
Australia Locked Bag 1, Footscray, Vic 3011
☎ 03 8379 8000  fax 03 8379 8111
e talk2us@lonelyplanet.com.au
USA      150 Linden St, Oakland, CA 94607
☎ 510 893 8555  Toll Free 800 275 8555
fax 510 893 8572
e info@lonelyplanet.com
UK       10a Spring Place, London NW5 3BH
☎ 020 7428 4800  fax 020 7428 4828
e go@lonelyplanet.co.uk
France   1 rue du Dahomey, 75011 Paris
☎ 01 55 25 33 00  fax 01 55 25 33 01
e bip@lonelyplanet.fr
www.lonelyplanet.fr

Designer Sonya Brooke Editor Rebecca Hobbs Proofer
Anne Mulvaney Cartographers Kusnandar and Jack
Gavran Cover Designer Maria Vallianos Project
Manager Charles Rawlings-Way Commissioning Editor
Michael Day Series Designer Gerilyn Attebery Series
Publishing Managers Katrina Browning and Diana Saad
Thanks to Corrine Waddell, David Burnett, Gabrielle
Green, Jane Thompson, Michelle Lewis, Quentin Frayne, LPI

Photographs
Photography by Phil Weymouth. Other photos as
indicated. Images also used with kind permission of
the Hong Kong Tourism Board.

Many of the photographs in this guide are available
for licensing from Lonely Planet Images:
e www.lonelyplanetimages.com

Front cover photographs
Top High-rise buildings and the harbour, seen from
Victoria Peak (Richard I'Anson)
Bottom Modern architecture in the Admiralty district –
the Lippo Centre (Frank Carter)

ISBN 1 74059 296 4

Text & maps © Lonely Planet Publications Pty Ltd 2003
Photos © photographers as indicated 2003
Printed through Colorcraft Ltd, Hong Kong
Printed in China

# how to use this book

## SYMBOLS

- ✉ address
- ☎ telephone number
- e email/website address
- Ⓜ nearest MTR (subway) station
- 🚋 tram access
- 🚌 nearest bus route
- 🚉 nearest train station
- ⛴ nearest ferry wharf
- ◷ opening hours
- ⓘ tourist information
- ⑤ cost, entry charge
- ♿ wheelchair access
- 👶 child-friendly
- ✕ on-site or nearby eatery
- Ⓥ good vegetarian selection

## COLOUR-CODING

Each chapter has a different colour code which is reflected on the maps for quick reference (eg all Highlights are bright yellow on the maps).

## MAPS

The fold-out maps inside the front and back covers are numbered from 1 to 7. All sights and venues in the text have map references that indicate where to find them on the maps; eg (4, E6) means Map 4, grid reference E6. Although each item is not pin-pointed on the maps, the street address is always indicated.

## PRICES

Price gradings (eg $10/5) usually indicate adult/concession entry charges to a venue. Concession prices can include child, senior and/or student discounts.

## AUTHOR AUTHOR!

**Patrick Witton**

Patrick cut his teeth as an editor for Lonely Planet's *World Food* series, then used them to research *World Food Indonesia*. The teeth got another workout in Hong Kong where he munched through a high-rise pile of dim sum. Patrick lives in Healesville where he writes for Vandal Press and plays banjo for a band called Cousin Dad.

Thanks to Miryana Power and all at HKTB, Dani Valent, Martin Hughes, John Batten, Donna Chan, Sindy Lai, Charlie Lai, Paul Benn, Steve Fallon, Gabrielle Green, Michael Day, Charles Rawlings-Way and to Rachel Blake who endorsed my Hong Kong explorations even when it meant being away for her birthday.

## READER FEEDBACK

Things change – prices go up, schedules change, good places go bad and bad places improve or go bankrupt. So, if you find things better or worse, recently opened or long since closed, please tell us and help make the next edition even more accurate. Send all correspondence to the Lonely Planet office closest to you (listed on page 2) or visit e www.lonelyplanet.com/feedback.

# facts about hong kong

This is Hong Kong: your mobile phone rings while you're shopping for dried fish stomach at a cluttered stall shadowed by a gleaming skyscraper. Or: you're eating bird's nest soup next to a woman wearing a chic anti-pollution face mask, a cutesy hairbow and a T-shirt that reads 'Hysteric Glamour'. This is Hong Kong too: you're heading upstairs with a stomach full of tea and cake when the concierge glides up to say your suit is ready for the second fitting. And later: you're celebrating the closing of a deal with colleagues at a seafood restaurant with a prime harbour view and you're managing the chopsticks like a professional.

Hong Kong has the big city specials like smog, odour, 14 million elbows and an insane love of clatter. But it's also efficient, hushed and peaceful: the transport network is excellent, the shopping centres are sublime and the temples and quiet corners of parks are contemplative oases.

It's an intoxicating place, spectacular, exotic and accessible. The food is fantastic, the shopping is great, there are some terrific hotels, doing business is a breeze and there's a surprising range of nature-loving getaways within easy reach. If you're visiting for business, you'll find pleasure sneaking up on you; if you're visiting for pleasure, there are thousands of locals who make it their business to please.

*The view from the famous glass curtain of the Convention & Exhibition Centre*

# HISTORY

Before Britain claimed Hong Kong, it was a neglected corner of the Qing dynasty (1644-1911) empire inhabited by farmers, fishermen and pirates. Trade between China and Britain commenced in 1685 but the balance was in favour of China until the British started trading opium to the Chinese in the late 18th century.

Chinese Emperor Dao Guang soon banned opium but illegal trade continued until 1839, when mandarin Lin Zexu destroyed 20,000 chests of the 'foreign mud'. British Foreign Secretary Lord Palmerston ordered his navy to force open the closed doors of Chinese trade. The British blockaded Guangzhou and then sailed north, forcing the Chinese to negotiate. Captain Charles Elliot, the chief superintendent of trade, demanded that a small, hilly island near the Pearl River estuary be ceded 'in perpetuity'. As Elliot saw it, this could be the British Empire's outpost in the Far East.

### Land Grab Gag

'Albert is so amused at my having got the island of Hong Kong,' wrote Queen Victoria to King Leopold of Belgium in 1841. While her husband could see the funny side of this apparently useless little island off the south coast of China, Lord Palmerston was less amused. He considered the acquisition of Hong Kong a massive bungle. 'A barren island with hardly a house upon it!' he raged in a letter to the man responsible for the deal, Captain Charles Elliot.

Hong Kong formally became a British possession on 26 June 1843. The Second Anglo-Chinese War in 1860 gave the British the Kowloon peninsula, and 40 years later they also claimed the New Territories. Instead of annexing the land outright, they agreed to a 99-year lease. The countdown to British Hong Kong's expiration had begun.

Steady numbers of Chinese refugees entered the colony during the 1920s and 30s, but in 1941 Japan swept in and occupied the territory for four years.

The communist revolution in 1949 sent refugees pouring into Hong Kong and the city was reinvented as an immense manufacturing and financial centre. By the end of the 1950s Hong Kong–made textiles, watches and basic electronics had turned the colony into an unlikely economic powerhouse. From a population of 600,000 people in 1945, Hong Kong was home to around three million by 1960.

China was not a shy and retiring neighbour. In 1962 it opened the border gates, allowing 70,000 people to flood into the colony in a few weeks. In 1967, at the height of the Cultural Revolution, riots inspired by the Red Guards rocked the colony. Panic spread but Hong Kong's colonial masters held their ground and Hong Kong got on with the business of getting rich.

*Has it come to this, comrade?*

During the 1970s, Taiwan, South Korea and Singapore began to mimic Hong Kong's success. Just as their cheap labour was threatening to undermine Hong Kong manufacturers, China under Deng Xiaoping opened up the country to tourism and foreign investment. Trade in Hong Kong skyrocketed as it became a transhipment point for China.

Few people gave much thought to Hong Kong's future until the early 1980s, when the British and Chinese governments started meeting to decide what would happen come 1997. Though Britain was legally bound to hand back only the New Territories, it would have been an awkward division. In December 1984 the British formally agreed to hand back the entire colony in 1997. A joint declaration theoretically allowed the 'Hong Kong Special Administrative Region (SAR) of China' to retain its social, economic and legal systems for at least 50 years after 1997. In 1988 Beijing published the Basic Law for Hong Kong, enshrining rights to property, travel, trade and free speech.

Bed linen & boardrooms: Hong Kong Island

Though China insists that the Basic Law is the Hong Kong people's guarantee of the good life, Beijing's actions since have given Hong Kongers cause to worry. Chief among these was the Tiananmen Square massacre of 4 June 1989 after which confidence plummeted in Hong Kong and capital headed overseas.

In 1996 Beijing-led elections were held for the position of chief executive, a new position created under the Basic Law. Shipping tycoon Tung Chee Hwa was the predictable choice: he's the acceptable face of China to Hong Kong, being a speaker of Cantonese and English, and an expert businessman.

As the handover drew near, panic gave way to pragmatism. On the night of 30 June 1997, the last governor, Chris Patten, sailed away, the new rulers perused their domain and the expected political storm didn't eventuate.

Questions of political and social stability aside, Hong Kong was embroiled in the financial chaos that besieged Southeast Asia in 1998. Though not as robust as it has been, Hong Kong is still a vibrant financial centre and one of the world's great cities. China's official policy with regard to Hong Kong is 'one country, two systems', with a common view being that as long as Hong Kong continues to make money (and little noise) its autonomy is assured. But a number of crucial interventions by Chinese authorities in Hong Kong's affairs have made it evident that Hong Kong is not quite as autonomous as the slogan suggests.

# ORIENTATION

Hong Kong is comprised of Hong Kong Island (80 sq km) to the south, the mainland peninsula of Kowloon (47 sq km) to the north, and the New Territories (796 sq km) which sprawl north to mainland China. Hong Kong's 234 islands (175 sq km) are also part of the New Territories. Surprisingly, a good deal of Hong Kong is mountainous and sparsely inhabited. Around 40% of the territory is dedicated country parks.

The city itself is centred around Victoria Harbour. The main business district is Central, on Hong Kong Island. East of Central lies the Admiralty commercial district; Wan Chai, known for restaurants and clubs; then Causeway Bay, a major shopping area. Towering above it all is the Peak, an exclusive residential district. In Kowloon, Tsim Sha Tsui, Jordan and Yau Ma Tei are busy hotel and shopping areas, while Mong Kok is a bustling residential and shopping area. See pages 31-3 for more details.

### Dirty Deeds

In an attempt to clean up the city at street level, Hong Kong's Environmental Protection Department is hitting people where it hurts: the wallet. All over Hong Kong you'll see posters warning that spitting, littering, sticking up flyers and letting your doggy do the do will cost you $600. It has been an effective campaign, however some offenders have attacked police after being fined for a single 'expulsion'. Police are now receiving extra self-defence training to deal with spitting subversives.

*Think twice before you drop that...*

# ENVIRONMENT

It wasn't until the late 1980s that Hong Kong authorities decided to do something about their territory becoming a densely populated cesspool. The Environmental Protection Department has to deal with decades of serious environmental abuse and a population that hasn't been educated about the implications of littering and pollution.

Hong Kong's waterways and air are terribly polluted. Victoria Harbour has been treated as a sewer while smoke-belching factories, ceaseless construction and diesel vehicles have made the air a misery to breathe. Animals that have survived, such as pink dolphins and protected birds, are struggling.

Not all of Hong Kong is ravaged though: 21 country parks are protected from development, and all 17 reservoirs lie within their boundaries. Other positive signs include campaigns against littering and pollution, monitoring of beaches for disease-causing bacteria, introduction of electric buses and more recycling bins. However, these are minor initiatives given the 18,000 tonnes of domestic, industrial and construction waste generated *each day* in Hong Kong.

## GOVERNMENT & POLITICS

The overarching framework is Beijing's Basic Law, which bestows freedom on Hong Kong except in foreign affairs. But Hong Kong is not politically democratic. Business governs the territory; the democratic elements that exist are limited and the people are largely apolitical.

The executive branch of power is led by the chief executive. The chief executive is supported by an Executive Council; a financial secretary, responsible for the eco-nomic policies of the government;

*The right of assembly is guaranteed by law*

and the secretary for justice, responsible for drafting legislation.

The Legislative Council makes and debates laws and controls public expenditure. An independent judiciary administers justice and interprets the law.

Post-colonial Hong Kong has subtly changed. The territory has become more executive-led, turning the Legislative Council into little more than a rubber stamp. Furthermore, the civil service is becoming less accountable, prompting fears that the corruption that dogged it in the past will return.

## ECONOMY

Business is Hong Kong's heart and soul. Despite the economic catastrophe of late 1997, Hong Kong is still a capitalist's dream: free enterprise and trade, very low taxes, a hard-working labour force and excellent telecom-munications. The maximum personal income tax is 15%, and the corpor-ate profits tax is capped at 16.5%.

Service industries employ more than 75% of Hong Kong's work-force and make up nearly 80% of its GDP. Much of the services sector is underpinned by trade; Hong Kong is the world's eighth-largest trading entity.

China is Hong Kong's largest trading partner, supplying a third of the territory's total imports and exports. The USA, Japan, Germany and the UK are also large markets.

### Did You Know?

Buy it, eat it, drive it...per capita, Hong Kong's 7.3 million people make the most of the following:
- mobile phones
- Rolls Royces
- seafood
- horse betting
- cognac
- fur coats
- oranges

Hong Kong maintained average GDP growth of 5% through the 1990s and peaked at 10% in 2000, keeping inflation and the cost of living high. A slowdown to 2.1% occurred during 2001 but with exports increasing, GDP should grow to about 4.8% in 2003. Nevertheless, unemployment remains an issue as manufacturing and menial services are squeezed by restructures and modernisation.

# SOCIETY & CULTURE

While Hong Kong is very Westernised, Chinese beliefs and traditions dominate. Buddhism and Taoism are the main religions, though Confucianism, ancestor worship, animist beliefs and other religions have been incorporated into the milieu. Generally the Chinese are much less concerned with high-minded philosophies than they are with the pursuit of worldly success, the appeasement of spirits and prophecies about the future. Visits to temples are usually made for specific issues such as a relative's health or the success of a business.

## Take a Number

According to *fung shui,* the last number of your hotel room or airline seat can have great influence on your fortune. Look at the last number on your boarding pass or reservation and hope for the best:

1  neutral
2  illness
3  conflict
4  sex and romance
5  misfortune
6  legal trouble
7  good luck
8  prosperity
9  eternity

*Who's up for some number four?*

**Fortune-telling**  The most popular method of divination in Hong Kong is using 'fortune sticks' (p. 37) at a Buddhist or Taoist temple or altar.

**Fung Shui**  Literally meaning 'wind-water', *fung shui* aims to balance the elements of nature to create a harmonious environment. It's been in practice since the 12th century, and continues to influence the design of buildings, highways, parks, tunnels and grave sites. To guard against evil spirits, who can move only in straight lines, doors are often positioned at an angle. For similar reasons, beds cannot face doorways. Ideally, homes and businesses should have a view of calm water (even a fish tank helps). Corporate heads shouldn't have offices that face

*Filial piety: in Chinese temples, incense sticks are offered with prayers for the dead*

west: otherwise profits go the same direction as the setting sun. Houses often have small *fung shui* objects placed in rooms, such as two dragons coiled up opposite the door, or two lions facing the windows.

**The year of the…**
**Sheep** (2003), **Monkey** (2004), **Rooster** (2005), **Dog** (2006), **Pig** (2007)

**Chinese Zodiac** It is said that the animal year chart originated when Buddha commanded all animals to assemble before him. The calendar was established according to the order of arrival of the first 12 (there's no cat year, as the rat tricked it into arriving late). Being born or married in a particular year is believed to determine one's fortune, so parents often plan for their children's sign.

**Taijiquan** Literally meaning 'fist of the supreme ultimate', this slow-motion martial art has been popular for centuries, especially among older folk. The movements develop breathing muscles, promote digestion and improve muscle tone. It seems to work: there are some pretty sprightly old folk out there.

### Etiquette – Don't Do & Do Do

On the whole Hong Kong people are flexible, considerate and forgiving, especially if you are a visitor. Nevertheless, here are some pointers that will make things more comfortable for everyone:

**Clothing** Beyond the be-suited realm of business, casual dress is acceptable even at swish restaurants, but save your bikini for the beach and keep your thongs/flip-flops in the hotel.
**Giving & Getting** Always use two hands, whether giving your business card or lifting a fridge.
**Business Cards** In business circles a business card is a must. People simply won't take you seriously unless you have one (be sure to offer it with both hands). Bilingual cards can usually be printed within 24hrs; try printers along Man Wa Lane, Central or ask your hotel to direct you.
**China** Don't diss it, you're in it.
**Face** Think status and respect (receiving *and* showing): keep your cool, be polite and buy a designer apartment with a harbour view.
**Beach** Topless is a turnoff, nude is a no-no.
**Gifts** If you want to give flowers, chocolates or wine to someone (a fine idea if invited to their home) they may appear reluctant for fear of seeming greedy but insist and they'll give in.
**Colour Coding** Red symbolises good luck, virtue and wealth (but writing in red can convey anger); white symbolises death so think twice before giving white flowers.
**Mobile Phones** Whether you're dining or proposing marriage, if your phone rings answer it.

For dining etiquette see page 70.

# ARTS

Mention art in relation to Hong Kong, and the term 'cultural desert' will likely soon grace the conversation. It's not an altogether fair description. Granted, in this economy-minded city the arts tend to take a back seat, but the arts still flourish. See pages 87-90 for listings and venue information.

## Film – Honkywood

Once thought the bastion of trashy violence, Hong Kong's film industry has become the talk of Tinseltown. Gravity-defying fight scenes and Bruce Lee–esque conflict resolution were once considered a cinematic joke, and in 1999 things were looking grim for Hong Kong cinema due to the financial crisis and a boom in piracy. But it all changed when Ang Lee's *Crouching Tiger, Hidden Dragon* won an Oscar for best foreign film in 2001. Now Hong Kong–style fight scenes are *de rigueur* in Hollywood and local actors such as Jackie Chan and Chow Yun-Fat are in high demand. A small yet productive independent film industry exists in Hong Kong churning out around 100 films each year, including local hits such as Fruit Chan Goh's *Hollywood Hong Kong,* filmed in the ramshackle housing areas of Diamond Hill. The annual Hong Kong International Film Festival brings hundreds of films and is now one of the world's major film festivals.

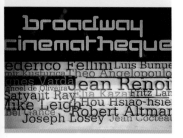

**Architecture** Architecture enthusiasts will find Hong Kong Island's Central and Wan Chai districts a fascinating showcase for the modern and postmodern. The Bank of China Tower (p. 20), the Hongkong & Shanghai Bank Building, the Lippo Centre, Exchange Square, the Convention & Exhibition Centre and The Center (pp. 35-7) are all impressive and very photogenic.

Progress has been made at the expense of history. Almost the only examples of pre-colonial Chinese architecture left in urban Hong Kong are the Tin Hau Temple, Tin Hau (p. 37) and the village house at the Law Uk Folk Museum (p. 34). There are temples and walled villages in Kowloon and the New Territories. Kowloon Walled City Park (p. 41) is one example.

Colonial architecture is also in short supply. Remnants include the Legislative Council Building (p. 36) and Stanley's Murray House (p. 49).

**Chinese Opera** Chinese opera is a world away from the Western variety. It is a mixture of singing, speaking, mime, acrobatics and dancing that lasts six hours. The main types of Chinese opera performed in Hong Kong are Beijing and Cantonese (p. 89). Beijing opera is highly refined, using almost no scenery. Cantonese is more like music-hall theatre with romance themes.

Costumes, props and body language reveal much of the meaning in Chinese opera – the Hong Kong Tourism Board's (HKTB's) *Hong Kong's*

*Musical Heritage* – Chinese Opera handout makes things easier to understand and enjoy. There's also an enlightening display on Cantonese opera at the Hong Kong Heritage Museum (p. 34).

**Dance** One Chinese tradition that lives on in Hong Kong is the lion dance. An acrobatic dance group under an elaborately painted Chinese lion costume leaps around among firecrackers and banging cymbals. Hong Kong's professional dance companies are: Hong Kong Dance Company (Chinese traditional); City Contemporary Dance Company (modern); and Hong Kong Ballet (classical and modern).

*Grand and gaudy: Chinese opera*

**Music** Classical music is alive and well in Hong Kong. The city boasts Chinese, philharmonic and chamber orchestras and a sinfonietta. Overseas performers of world repute frequently make it to Hong Kong, especially during February's Hong Kong Arts Festival.

Cantopop (p. 94) dominates the popular music scene.

**Painting** Painting in Hong Kong falls into three broad categories: contemporary local, classical Chinese and Western. Contemporary local art differs enormously from that of mainland China, as Hong Kong artists are largely the offspring of refugees and the products of cultural fusion; they blend East and West and are concerned with finding their orientation in the metropolis through personal statement. The best places to get your fix are the Hong Kong Museum of Art (p. 34), Para/Site Art Space (p. 39), John Batten Gallery (p. 39) and the Macau Museum of Art (p. 53).

**Theatre** Nearly all theatre is Western in form, but is staged in Cantonese. Theatre groups include The Hong Kong Repertory Theatre and The Hong Kong Academy for Performing Arts.

## Sculpture on the Streets

| | | |
|---|---|---|
| Henry Moore | *Oval with Points* | Exchange Square (4, D6) |
| Zhu Ming | *Taiji* | Exchange Square (4, D6) |
| Henry Moore | *Double Oval* | Jardine House (4, D6) |
| Cheung Yee | *copper reliefs* | Mandarin Oriental Hotel (4, E6) |
| Cezar | *The Flying Frenchman* | Hong Kong Cultural Centre (3, K4) |

# highlights

The best thing about being in Hong Kong is being in Hong Kong. It's about soaking up the atmosphere, being buzzed by the energy, getting flummoxed and fired by the confluences and contradictions of a city with multi-Asian and Western elements. It's about savouring new tastes, threading your way through human gridlock and realising you're humming some dumb Cantopop tune as you slurp your noodles.

Bona fide sights aren't exactly where it's at: once you've been up the Peak and crossed the harbour on a ferry, you've pretty much done the must-dos. But while you're picking off our other highlights, you're sure to hit upon some of the random greats that make Hong Kong the exuberant delight that it is.

## Stopping Over?

**One Day** Catch a tram up the Peak for a good gawk at the city. Stretch your legs on a summit circuit before lunching at the Peak Lookout. Return to sea level and jump a tram to Sheung Wan for shopping at Cat St and the Western Market. Take a tram back to Cyrano's bar and watch the sun go down.

**Two Days** Take the Star Ferry to Tsim Sha Tsui and visit the art, space or history museums. Have a dim sum brunch at The Sweet Dynasty, then browse Nathan Rd until you're hungry enough for afternoon tea at The Peninsula. Wander up Temple St for the night market, snacking on street food as the need arises.

**Three Days** Explore Central/Soho's shops, galleries and fashion stores via the escalator. Have a tapas lunch and watch the foot traffic at Boca on Peel St. Take a tram to Wan Chai for a night of Chinese opera or theatre at the Hong Kong Arts Centre. Strut your stuff at a Wan Chai bar before dining late at 369 Shanghai.

## Lowlights

Don't let minor gripes spoil your adventures…

**Crowds** Hordes bear down on every street, and if you're in a hurry everyone walks in front of you
**remember:** Duck into cafes and shops whenever respite is needed

**Pollution** Could there be more cars and trucks than trees?
**remember:** Take public transport and enjoy the pollution-induced sunset

**Rudeness** You're only asking directions but you're waved away like a fly
**remember:** For every rude person in Hong Kong there are 147,693 polite people willing to help

**Drips** Even when it's not pouring, the city's one million air-conditioners drip on your head
**remember:** They're cooling you down, inside and out

**Aberdeen** The boat dwellers are now in high-rise apartments and the Jumbo Floating Restaurant is a rip-off
**remember:** You can still get on the water in a hired sampan

**MTR** There's always a battle to get the few seats on the train
**remember:** It's so efficient you'll be at your destination before you can say 'mind the gap'

# TSIM SHA TSUI PROMENADE (3)

Stretching along one of the greatest harbours in the world, the Tsim Sha Tsui promenade offers some of the best views in Hong Kong. Undoubtedly the best time to take a promenade perambulation is at night, when the view of Central lit up like a million Chinese lanterns is nothing short of mesmerising. Some nights half of Hong Kong makes their way down to enjoy the neon-saturated scenery. You'll find yourself accompanied by joggers, lovers, musicians, families, insistent fortune tellers (keep walking) and people fishing right off the walkway. There's a raised area near the Clock Tower but stay with the crowds for the full experience. Professional photographers line up along the promenade offering to take poster-size portraits to capture the moment.

**INFORMATION**

- ⊠ south of Salisbury Rd along Victoria Harbour, Tsim Sha Tsui
- 🚢 Star Ferry, Tsim Sha Tsui East
- Ⓜ Tsim Sha Tsui
- Ⓢ free
- ♿ good
- ✕ Tsim Sha Tsui (pp. 81-3)

The promenade becomes a sea of people during the Chinese New Year fireworks displays in late January or early February, and again in June during the Dragon Boat Festival. You can walk along the water from the Star Ferry terminal all the way to the Hong

*Beneath the eaves of the Cultural Centre*

Kong Coliseum and Kowloon KCR terminal. Midway along the promenade is a ferry pier where you can catch a hovercraft to Hong Kong Island.

During the day the view is still stunning, but the heat or pollution can sap you (especially during summer). Luckily the **Hong Kong Museum of Art** (p. 34), the **Space Museum & Theatre** (p. 38) and the **Hong Kong Cultural Centre** (p. 36) are all on the promenade so mid-mooch you can duck in for a shaded change of scene.

### Walking on Water

Hong Kong isn't what it used to be, it's more. Much of the land covered in the Tsim Sha Tsui promenade has been 'reclaimed' from the continually shrinking Victoria Harbour. In the past decade or so Hong Kong's surface area has grown about 3% due to land reclamation.

# VICTORIA PEAK (2, C2)

First clear day, get your booty up here: if you haven't been to the Peak, then you haven't been to Hong Kong. Not only is the view one of the most spectacular cityscapes in the world, it's also a good way to get Hong Kong into perspective. Repeat the trip up on a not-too-murky night, as the illuminated outlook is superb.

The Peak has been *the* place to live ever since the British moved in. The taipans built summer houses here to escape the heat and humidity (it's usually about 5°C cooler than down below). The Peak is still the most fashionable place to live in Hong Kong, as reflected by the astronomical real estate prices and bumper-to-bumper luxury traffic.

This being Hong Kong, there's a four-level shopping plaza plonked up here (the overblown, overpriced **Peak Galleria**) along with the **Peak Tower**, which resembles a huge titanium anvil and holds theme entertainment, shops, restaurants and the Peak Tram terminal.

When people refer to the Peak, they generally mean this plateau (400m) and the surrounding residential area. Victoria Peak (552m) is actually the summit – about 500m to the west up steep Mt Austin Rd. The **old governor's mountain lodge** is near the summit. The lodge was burnt to the ground by the Japanese during WWII, but the gardens remain and are open to the public.

You can walk around Victoria Peak without exhausting yourself. Harlech Rd is on the south side while Lugard Rd is on the north slope and together they form a 3.5km loop. The walk takes about an hour and is lit

| **DON'T MISS** | • riding the Peak Tram • an ice cream on the viewing deck<br>• walking to the top of the hill • finding your hotel on the skyline |
| --- | --- |

*Like New York and Paris, Hong Kong demands to be surveyed from a great height*

at night. If you feel like a longer walk, you can continue for a further 2km along Peak Rd to Pok Fu Lam Reservoir Rd, which leaves Peak Rd near the car park exit. This goes past the reservoir to the main Pok Fu Lam Rd, where you can get the No 7 bus to Aberdeen or back to Central.

Another good walk is down to Hong Kong University (2, C1). First walk to the west side of Victoria Peak by taking either Lugard or Harlech Rds. After reaching Hatton Rd, follow it down. The descent is very steep but the path is obvious.

The Peak is a good place to bring the kids: You'll find the **Peak Explorer** (a futuristic ride in space and time), **Ripley's Believe it or Not! odditorium**, an outpost of Madame Tussaud's, the children-friendly **Restaurant Marché** (p. 84) and a **viewing terrace** with coin-operated binoculars. There are whispers that a bungy-jump will soon operate from the top of the anvil.

You should catch the **Peak Tram** (p. 111) at least one way. It's such a steep ride that the floor is angled to help standing passengers stay upright. Running for more than 100 years, the tram has never had an accident – a comforting thought if you start to have doubts about the strength of the cable. In 1885 everyone thought the Honourable Phineas Kyrie and William Kerfoot Hughes were crazy when they announced their intention to build a tramway to the top, but it opened three years later, wiping out the scoffers and the sedan-chair trade in one go. Since

## INFORMATION

- Peak Tram, Garden Rd, Central (p. 111) Note: the Central Escalator doesn't go to the Peak
- 15 (from Exchange Sq), minibus 1 (from Star Ferry)
- $ free
- e www.thepeak.com.hk
- Peak Tram ☎ 2522 0922, Ripley's Believe it or Not! odditorium ☎ 2849 0818
- good (not tram)
- ✕ Peak Lookout, Cafe Deco, Restaurant Marché (p. 84)

*The Peak Lookout: a favourite with visitors*

then, the tram has been stopped only by WWII and the violent rainstorms of 1966, which washed half the track down the hillside. The tram terminal is on Garden Rd, Central, at the northwestern corner of Hong Kong Park, 650m from the Star Ferry terminal.

# HONG KONG MUSEUM OF HISTORY (3, E7)

Commercial Hong Kong has all eyes on the future but when you see a computer salesman tending the shrine in his shop, you get an inkling that much of the city's character lies in its past. To gain a deeper understanding of this intriguing city, you have to hang with its ancestors and get in the cupboard with its skeletons: thus a visit to this new museum is almost essential.

Purpose-built in Tsim Sha Tsui East, the history museum takes the visitor on a fascinating walk through the area's past, from prehistoric times (about 6000 years ago, give or take a lunar year) right through to the fast-talking present. Landform, climate, geology, flora and fauna are covered (some of the stuffed animals are looking a bit wonky) before the human stories get a look in. There are replicas of village dwellings, traditional Chinese costumes and a realistic re-creation of an entire street block from 1881, including an old Chinese medicine shop.

The large collection of 19th- and early-20th-century photographs is very atmospheric but our favourite is the mosh of toys and collectibles from the 1960s and 70s when 'Made in Hong Kong' meant 'Christmas stocking trash'. Overall, the museum does a fine job of relaying the fascinating story of Hong Kong.

## INFORMATION

- ✉ 100 Chatham Rd, Tsim Sha Tsui East
- ☎ 2724 9042
- Ⓔ Tsim Sha Tsui, Jordan
- 🚌 5C, 8
- 🕐 Mon & Wed-Sat 10am-6pm, Sun 10am-7pm
- ⑤ $10/5 (free Wed)
- 🖥 www.lcsd.gov.hk /hkmh/
- ♿ good
- ✗ Fruit Shop (p. 83)

---

**DON'T MISS**
- multimedia presentations from Stone Age to Cyber Age • Ming Dynasty, Opium Wars and Japanese Occupation galleries • gawking at school kids as they gawk at Neanderthals

*From junks to Neolithic pile-drivers, the museum is a showcase of Hong Kong industry*

# STAR FERRY                     (3, K3 & 4, D7)

Since 1898, gutsy double-decker ferries have chugged back and forth between Kowloon and Hong Kong Island. Over the decades land reclamation has made the journey marginally shorter, while rampant development has turned it into one of the most spectacular commutes imaginable. There's something nice about doing what's on every tourist's A-list and finding that the gawping shutterbugs are outnumbered by blasé newspaper readers. Morning and evening, Star Ferries are a common way for the locals to hop from island to mainland and back again.

**INFORMATION**
- ☎ 2366 2576
- ⊘ 6.30am-11pm
- $ $1.70/2.20 lower/upper deck (65 years of age and over free), exact change needed
- ♿ fair
- ✗ City Hall Chinese Restaurant (p.72)

Though the ferries have names like *Morning Star*, *Evening Star* and *Celestial Star*, most of their traffic is through the starless daylight. It's at night though that the romance of the ferries comes to the fore: the boats are festively strung with lights, the city buildings beam an evening rainbow onto the rippling water, the energy of the day has eased and canoodling appears the only sensible thing to do.

There are four Star Ferry routes, but by far the most popular is the run between Tsim Sha Tsui and Central. The trip takes 7mins (they invite you to time it), and there are departures every 5 to 10mins.

### Waterborne War Hero
During the Japanese invasion, the Star Ferries became something of a saviour when the boats were used to evacuate refugees and Allied troops from The Peninsula.

*If you haven't done the Star Ferry, you haven't done Hong Kong*

# BANK OF CHINA TOWER                    (4, F7)

Still the architectural symbol of Hong Kong, this 74-storey building was completed in 1990. Impressive as it is, the building is very much a brash and hard-edged synopsis of the 1980s. It had to be bigger than the nearby Hongkong & Shanghai Bank Building (p. 36), as it represented the new power in town, the People's Republic of China. Though it's not the tallest building in Hong Kong (that honour goes to the new IFC Tower, see page 35), the Bank of China Tower still manages to dominate the skyline.

**INFORMATION**

- ✉ 1 Garden Rd, Central
- Ⓜ Admiralty, Central
- ⏲ bank: Mon-Fri 9am-4.30pm, Sat 9am-12.30pm; lobby: 24hrs
- Ⓢ free
- ♿ good
- ✗ Vong (p. 73), Mix (p. 72)

Despite being designed by Chinese-born architect Ieoh Ming Pei, the building is clearly Western in inspiration. Chinese elements are incorporated but muted. Many locals see the building as a huge violation of *fung shui* principles. For example, according to *fung shui* the bank's four triangular prisms are negative symbols; being the opposite to circles, these contradict what circles suggest – money, perfection and prosperity. Furthermore, the building's shape has been likened to a praying mantis (unsurprisingly, considered a threatening symbol), as the radio masts look like insect's antennae. Even more sinister are the triangular angles on the surface of the building – these are associated with daggers or blades and it is claimed they cut into neighbouring buildings.

Take the express lift to the 43rd floor from where you'll be rewarded with a panoramic view over Hong Kong. From here you are about the same height as the Hongkong & Shanghai Bank Building. It's rather a pity that you aren't allowed to go any higher, as it is exciting swaying with the wind at the top.

## Rubik's Diamond?

The puzzling asymmetry of the building is in reality a simple geometric exercise. Rising from the ground like a cube, it is successively reduced, quarter by quarter, until the south-facing quarter is left to rise ever upwards.

*One diamond that needs constant polishing*

# HONG KONG TRAMS                    (4 & 5)

Hong Kong's slowest and least flashy mode of public transport is arguably its most fun. The 163 tottering trams comprise the only double-decker tramcar fleet in the world and, though they don't have the star appeal of the harbour ferries, the trams are endearingly antiquated and doggedly handy.

The first trams got going in 1904, running across the north of Hong Kong Island from Kennedy Town to Shau Kei Wan. The network has been augmented by seven other routes over the decades, all of them passing through Sheung Wan, Central and Admiralty, and some sheering off to loop around Happy Valley Racecourse.

When the trams first started running they caused multiple sensations: the stops were packed with people but not all of them wanted to go anywhere. A great number just jumped on, walked through having a gander and treading on toes, then

**INFORMATION**

☎ 2548 7102
Ⓑ Sheung Wan,
    Central, Admiralty,
    Wan Chai,
    Causeway Bay
🚢 Star Ferry
🕐 6am-1am
⑤ $2/1

## Tram Trade

Air-conditioners are everywhere in Hong Kong and are now making their way into the city's trams. For many this is a shame, as sealing up tram windows means blocking out passing sounds and smells, as well as the fine breeze that flows through the carriage while it trundles along.

got off again, not quite game to ride. The trams were also delayed by hawkers who took advantage of the tramway by dragging their heavy carts along the well-made tracks – eventually in 1911, a law was passed banning carts with the same wheel gauge as the trams. This law is still in effect today.

*Double-decker trams totter down Central*

# THE PENINSULA (3, J5)

More than a Hong Kong landmark, The Peninsula is one of the world's great hotels. Before WWII it was one of several prestigious hotels across Asia where anyone who was anyone stayed, lining up with the likes of the Raffles in Singapore and the Taj in Bombay.

*If you've got it, flaunt it at The Peninsula*

## INFORMATION

- ✉ cnr Salisbury & Nathan Rds, Tsim Sha Tsui
- ☎ 2920 2888
- Ⓗ Tsim Sha Tsui
- 🚢 Star Ferry
- ⏰ afternoon tea: 2-7pm
- 💲 afternoon tea: $180-220
- ⓔ www.peninsula.com
- ♿ excellent
- ✗ Gaddi's (p. 81), Felix (p. 81), Spring Moon (p. 82), afternoon tea in the Lobby

Land reclamation has robbed the hotel of its top waterfront location, but the new 20-storey extension still offers sweeping views of Hong Kong Island (or Kowloon from your spa). Even the breathtaking interior is worth a visit and there are many reasons to linger.

Taking **afternoon tea** at The Peninsula is one of the best experiences in town – dress neatly and be prepared to line up for a table. While you're waiting, you can listen to the string quartet and salivate at the sight of everyone else's cucumber sandwiches and dainty cakes. From 6pm, catch a dedicated lift up to **Felix** (p. 81), have a martini and gulp down the view. Stay for dinner or dress up for **Gaddi's** (p. 81), the most exclusive French restaurant in town.

If you're dilly-dallying on luxury hotel accommodation, plunge into **The Peninsula** (p. 102). Unprecedented care is taken to make sure your stay here is sublime, from fresh fruit and fine tea on arrival to making sure you have more bath robes than bodies.

## The Old & The New

The Peninsula turns 75 on 11 December 2003, and in pure Pen form, celebrations are already under way. Activities and events have already commenced and many will continue well beyond the birthday. Celebrations to look out for include the return of the traditional Sunday afternoon tea dance and historical walks, as well as ongoing artistic, musical and photographic projects.

**DON'T MISS**
- fine tea and nibbles in the Lobby • browsing the boutiques • asking to inspect one of the fab suites • using the men's loo at Felix (trust us)

# MAN MO TEMPLE                                    (4, D2)

This temple is one of the oldest and most famous in Hong Kong. The Man Mo (literally 'Civil and Military') is dedicated to two deities. The civil deity is a Chinese statesman of the 3rd century BC and the military deity is Kuanti, a soldier born in the 2nd century AD and now worshipped as the God of War. Also known as Kwan Tai or Kwan Kung, Kuanti's popularity in Hong Kong is probably more attributable to his status as the patron god of restaurants, pawn shops, the police force and secret societies such as the Triad organisations.

**INFORMATION**

- ✉ cnr Hollywood Rd & Ladder St, Sheung Wan
- 🚌 26
- 🕐 8am-6pm
- 💲 free
- ✕ Leung Hing Seafood Restaurant (p. 80)

Outside the entrance are four gilt plaques on poles that are carried at procession time. Two plaques describe the gods being worshipped; the others request quietness and respect and warn menstruating women to keep out of the main hall. Inside the temple are two antique chairs shaped like houses, used to carry the two gods at festival time. The coils suspended from the roof are incense cones burnt by worshippers. A large bell on the right is dated 1846 and the smaller ones on the left were made in 1897.

### Wong Hotel

The area around the temple was used for location shots in the film *The World of Suzie Wong*, based on the novel by Richard Mason. The building to the right of the temple appears as Suzie's hotel, although the real hotel Luk Kwok (called Nam Kok in the film and now rebuilt) is in Wan Chai.

The exact date of the temple's construction has never been agreed on, but it's certain it was already standing when the British arrived to claim the island. The present Man Mo Temple was renovated in the mid-19th century.

*Fine carvings and delicate curved eaves grace the Man Mo Temple*

# NATHAN RD (3, E5)

From the waterfront all the way north to the New Territories border, Nathan Rd is packed with hundreds of shops and hotels and people darting in and out of them. It's loud, crowded, relentless and, with dozens of

## INFORMATION

- Tsim Sha Tsui, Jordan, Yau Ma Tei, Mong Kok
- Star Ferry
- 1, 1A, 2, 6, 6A, 7
- Tsim Sha Tsui (pp. 81-3), Yau Ma Tei (p. 86), Mong Kok (p. 79)

*The famous neon signs of Nathan Rd*

### Chungking Mansions

This squalid high-rise budget accommodation ghetto at 36-44 Nathan Rd is a Hong Kong icon. Both backpackers and immigrants are regular residents of the labyrinthine hotel rooms, but with one look at the 'fire escape' you'll see why we wouldn't recommend staying here. Nevertheless the ground floor is a lively market of souvenir stalls, money changers and good Indian eateries. The mansions' infamy is fuelled by both tall and true tales of fires, crime and unclaimed bodies, and it featured in Wong Kar-Wai's fantastic 1994 film *Chungking Express*.

buses juddering along its length, rather asphyxiating. But the intoxicating mayhem of Nathan Rd typifies the vibrant Hong Kong consumer experience.

Kowloon's main drag was named after the governor, Sir Matthew Nathan, around the turn of the 20th century. It was promptly dubbed 'Nathan's Folly' since Kowloon at the time was sparsely populated and such a wide road was thought unnecessary. Nearly all the trees that once lined the street are gone (look for them at the front of Kowloon Park) but some would say the folly has remained.

The lower end of Nathan Rd is known as the **Golden Mile**, after both its sky-high real estate prices and its ability to suck money out of tourists' pockets. Seedy guesthouse ghettoes awkwardly rub shoulders with top-end hotels, Indian tailors ply their trade on street corners and every other person seems intent on divesting you of wads of cash.

**DON'T MISS**
- a drink at the Sheraton's Sky Lounge (p. 97) • high fashion at Joyce Ma (p. 59) • Chinese goodies at Yue Hwa (p. 68) • a trip to Kowloon Park (p. 41) • taking a double-decker bus back to the Star Ferry (p. 19)

# HONG KONG TRAIL                    (2, D3)

Hong Kong has a truly surprising number of walking trails. For those who like a challenge, it is possible to tramp the length of Hong Kong Island on the rugged 50km-long Hong Kong Trail. Starting from the Peak Tram terminal on Victoria Peak, the trail follows Lugard Rd to the west, and drops down the hill to Pok Fu Lam Reservoir, near Aberdeen, before turning east and zigzagging across the ridges. The trail traverses four country parks: **Pok Fu Lam Country Park** south of Victoria Peak; **Aberdeen Country Park** east of the Peak; **Tai Tam Country Park** on the east side of the island; and **Shek O Country Park** in the southeast. Tai Tam is the largest of these parks, and arguably the most beautiful with its dense emerald forests and trickling streams. The Hong Kong Trail skirts the northern side of the Tai Tam Reservoir, which is the largest lake on the island.

It's possible to hike the entire trail in one day, but most walkers pick a manageable section to suit. For the spectacular **Dragon's Back** section of the trail see the Shek O excursion (p. 51).

For more information, get a copy of the *Hong Kong Trail* map published by the Country & Marine Parks Authority (CPA) or *Exploring Hong Kong's Countryside* by Edward Stokes.

## INFORMATION

- 🚌 Pok Fu Lam section: 15 (from Exchange Sq to Victoria Peak); Tai Tam section: 6, 61 (from Exchange Sq to Wong Nai Chung Gap); Shek O section (p. 51)
- ⓘ CPA ☎ 2422 9431; Government Publications Centre, 66 Queensway, Admiralty ☎ 2537 1910
- 🄴 parks.afcd.gov.hk
- ♿ toilets & accessible BBQs at visitors centre, Aberdeen Country Park
- ✕ Peak Lookout (p. 84), Restaurant Marché (p. 84), Cafe Deco (p. 84)

*Revive your senses, stretch your legs and clear your mind*

**DON'T MISS**
• spectacular views over Shek O and the South China Sea • 200 species of butterfly • a spot of frog-spotting • 500-year-old lichen in Pok Fu Lam • barking deer in the Tai Tam Valley

# TEMPLE ST NIGHT MARKET (3, C4)

Temple St (named after the **Tin Hau Temple** at its centre, see page 37) is the liveliest night market in Hong Kong, and the place to go for cheap clothes, food, watches, pirated CDs, fake labels, footwear, cookware and everyday items. It used to be known as 'Men's St' because the market only sold men's clothing. Though there are still a lot of men's items on sale, vendors don't discriminate – anyone's money will do.

## INFORMATION

✉ Temple St, Yau Ma Tei
🚇 Yau Ma Tei, Jordan
🕐 6pm-midnight
   (best 8-11pm)
💲 free
✗ Yau Ma Tei (p. 86),
   Mong Kok (p. 79)

Any marked prices should be considered mere suggestions: this is definitely a place to bargain. You'll find the stall-holders tough negotiators though – if you're busting a gut over a couple of dollars, keep in mind that HK$1 is worth around US$0.10.

Temple St extends all the way from Man Ming Lane in the north to Ning Po St in the south, and is divided by Tin Hau Temple. For street food, head to northern Temple St. You can get anything from a simple bowl of noodles to a full meal, served at your very own table on the street. There are also a

*Placate the folks you left at home*

### Haggle Gaggle

Say *Peng didak m dak a?* (Can you reduce the price?) to start negotiations. If the stall-holder stays high (they'll probably tap it in on a calculator) say *Ho gwai* (That's very expensive!) and see if they'll budge.

few seafood and hotpot restaurants. Also on Temple St are all sorts of food stalls selling huge fried sausages *(heungcheung)* and fried kebabs with chicken *(gai)* and aubergine *(ayegwa)*. Do like the locals do: stand up and fortify yourself for the haggling ahead.

*Ho gwai!...for a fake Rolex*

# HONG KONG PARK (4, G7)

This is one of the most unusual parks in the world, deliberately designed to look anything but natural, and emphasising synthetic creations such as its fountain plaza, conservatory, aviary, artificial waterfall, indoor games hall, playground, viewing tower, museum and taijiquan garden.

For all its artifice, the park is beautiful in its own weird way and, with a wall of skyscrapers on one side and mountains on the other, makes for some dramatic photography.

Perhaps the best feature of the park is the **aviary**. Home to more than 800 birds (and 30 different species), the aviary is huge. To enter is to have the impression of wandering into a world of birds. Visitors walk along a wooden bridge suspended about 10m above the ground and on eyelevel with the tree branches, where most of the birds are to be found.

Also in the park is the **Flagstaff House Museum of Teaware** (p. 34). The building dates from 1846, making it the oldest Western-style structure in Hong Kong. Within the former Victoria Barracks, the **Hong Kong Visual Arts Centre** is a hirespace comprising 10 studios and a modest exhibition space showing a good range of ceramics, prints and

**INFORMATION**

✉ Cotton Tree Dr, Admiralty

🚇 Admiralty, Central

🚌 3, 12, 23

🕐 6.30am-11pm; conservatory & aviary: 9am-5pm; Hong Kong Visual Arts Centre: Wed-Mon 10am-9pm

$ free

♿ fair

✕ snack shops & restaurant on site

*A young skater spreads her wings*

sculpture mostly produced on site. The most tranquil area of the park is the **taijiquan garden**. It's busiest early in the morning when a sizable quotient of locals come to do their exercises but at any time of day you're likely to find someone standing in a pose or sitting in restful silence.

*A boy poses in the fountain plaza*

**DON'T MISS**
- steaming up in the conservatory • getting in a flap in the aviary
- more vegetation than construction • striking a pose in the taijiquan garden • letting the kids loose in the playground

# REPULSE BAY (2, D3)

The pleasures of Repulse Bay don't lie in the water (murky), the sea floor (slimy) or the long, greyish beach. What Repulse Bay excels in is holiday

**INFORMATION**

🚌 6, 6A, 61, 66, 260, 262
💲 free
🍴 The Verandah (p. 80)

atmosphere and people-watching, especially in summer when the beach is packed every day of the week.

Towards the eastern end of the beach is the unusual **Kwun Yum & Tin Hau Statues**, which front the ornate Life Saver's Club. The area is full of other statues and mosaics of Kwun Yum, the God of Mercy, and inside is the headquarters of the Royal Lifesaving Society. The sprawling temple houses an amazing assembly of deities and figures, including a four-faced Buddha and a posse of goats. Most of the statues were funded by local personalities and businessfolk during the 1970s, in a dual act of honour and kudos. Crossing the Longevity Bridge on the forecourt is supposed to add three days to your life (people walk back and forth to gain a month or two).

You can keep walking east and south to **Middle Bay** and **South Bay**, respectively about 10 and 30mins walk along the shore. These beaches are usually less crowded but not any cleaner.

Repulse Bay is home to some of Hong Kong's rich and famous: the pink, purple and yellow condos with a giant square cut out of the middle are The Repulse Bay, also home to the fancy restaurant **The Verandah** (p. 80) and an upscale shopping mall. Apparently this design feature was added at the behest of a *fung shui* expert, though such a stunt might also have been devised to push up the property's value.

**DON'T MISS** • walking along the beach • crossing the Longevity Bridge • afternoon tea at The Verandah • getting your picture taken by tourists from mainland China • watching couples pose for wedding photos

*Like a theme park of Chinese religion: Kwun Yum & Tin Hau Statues*

# HAPPY VALLEY RACECOURSE (5, J2)

Apart from mah jong games and the Mark Six Lottery, racing is the only form of legal gambling in Hong Kong. The first horse races were held in 1846 at Happy Valley Racecourse and became an annual event. Now there are about 75 meetings a year split between Happy Valley and the newer, larger track at Sha Tin in the New Territories. The racing season runs from September to June, with most races on Wednesday night.

If you've been in Hong Kong for less than 21 days you can get a tourist ticket. This is worthwhile, especially when the racecourse is crowded – at times up to 50,000 fans have been turned away! Tourist ticket-holders will be admitted despite the crowds – you can also walk around next to the finish area. Bring your passport to qualify.

Racing buffs can wallow in history at the **Hong Kong Racing Museum** on the 2nd floor of the Happy Valley Stand at the racecourse – it's open throughout the year.

Also of historical interest are the several **cemeteries** across Morrison Hill Rd. These are divided into Catholic, Protestant and Muslim sections and date to the founding of Hong Kong as a colony. The placement is somewhat ironic, as is Happy Valley's name, for the area was a malaria-infested bog that led to a fair number of fatalities before the swamps were drained. Many of the victims of the huge fire at Happy Valley Racecourse over 80 years ago are also buried there.

Hong Kong Tourism Board

## INFORMATION

- ✉ Wong Nai Chung Rd, Happy Valley
- ☎ 2966 7940
- 🚇 Happy Valley
- 🚌 1, 5A
- ⏱ races: Sept-June, Wed 7-11pm & weekends as scheduled; Hong Kong Racing Museum: Tues-Sat 10am-5pm, Sun 1-5pm
- 💲 races: $10-50; Hong Kong Racing Museum: free
- 🌐 www.happyvalley racecourse.com
- ⓘ Hong Kong Racing Museum
- ☎ 2966 8065
- ♿ good facilities including toilets & dedicated seating
- ✕ food stands on site

Hong Kong Tourism Board

### Sport Superstitions

You can hug them, kiss them, buy them a drink, but whatever you do don't slap or grab the shoulder of your fellow punter. Even in the euphoria of backing a winner you have to remember the forces of superstition, which state that 'shouldering affection' will bring bad luck to the slapped.

# TEN THOUSAND BUDDHAS MONASTERY (1, D7)

It may not be as grand as Indonesia's Borobudur, or as old as Cambodia's Angkor Wat, but the Ten Thousand Buddhas Monastery typifies Hong

**INFORMATION**

- 🚇 KCR Sha Tin
- 🕐 9am-5pm
- 💲 donations welcome
- 🌐 www.10kbuddhas.org
- 🍴 vegetarian restaurant at temple

Richard I'Anson

Kong for its deep spirituality, open opulence and more than a hint of absurdity. The monastery, founded in 1950, sits on a hillside about 500m northwest of Sha Tin KCR station. It's a relatively steep walk to the monastery grounds but you're rewarded with the experience of passing through Pai Tau (a traditional village), past pockets of lush forest and up to the 400 steps flanked by an avenue of life-size, character-rich golden Buddha statues. These statues mix and mingle up at the monastery grounds, some vividly displaying their abilities: there's the one with an extender arm; the tiger killer; and the blue doggy rider. As well as these glorious golden Buddhas, the grounds hold a nine-storey pagoda, ancestral worship room and urns where devotees burn incense, covering the monastery in a fragrant fog. From the grounds is a superb view of Sha Tin and nearby mountains.

### The Golden Guy

Within the main temple of the Ten Thousand Buddhas Monastery is the embalmed body of the monastery's founding member, who died in 1965. His body was encased in gold leaf and is now on display behind glass. Put a small donation in the box next to the display case to help pay for the temple's upkeep.

Ten Thousand Buddhas Monastery

On entering the main temple you'll discover the evidence behind the monastery's understated name: some 12,800 miniature statues line the towering walls of the room. Look closely and you'll discover the pose of each Buddha differs slightly. Back outside, another path encroached by Buddhas and vegetation meanders down from the eastern side of the main temple back to Sha Tin.

Richard I'Anson

# sights & activities

## NEIGHBOURHOODS
### Hong Kong Island

Though the island makes up only 7% of Hong Kong's land area, it is the territory's centre of gravity, and is home to most of the major businesses, government offices, top-end hotels and restaurants and upper-crust neighbourhoods. A great way to see the north side is to jump on one of the wobbly double-decker trams. The south side, where the beaches are, has a completely different feel.

**Aberdeen** was once a tourist attraction due to several thousand people living aboard anchored junks. Now the main draw is the floating restaurants (p. 80). To get close to the harbour action take a sampan tour, which can be arranged at the Aberdeen Promenade.

Just east of Central, **Admiralty** is a clump of office towers, hotels and shopping centres. There are no sights here, but the Pacific Place shopping mall (p. 61) is one of Hong Kong's nicest. Across Queensway, the Lippo Centre (pp. 36-7) makes an interesting addition to Hong Kong's skyline.

**Causeway Bay** is a shopping hub. Several shopping centres can be found south of Hennessy Rd, chief among them Times Square. People also visit Causeway Bay to eat and, to a lesser extent, pub-crawl. The consumer rush gives this district a vibrant feel at almost any time of the day or night.

### Off the Beaten Track
If the tourist trail is getting you down, it's possible to get away from it all – even in manic Hong Kong. These lesser-known attractions are good spots to chill out:

- Cattle Depot Artist Village (p. 39)
- Chi Lin Nunnery (p. 35)
- Hong Kong Heritage Museum (p. 34)
- Kowloon Walled City Park (p. 41)
- Lei Cheng Uk Museum & Han Tomb (p. 36)
- Ten Thousand Buddhas Monastery (p. 30)
- Tin Hau Temples (p. 37)
- Wishing Tree (p. 43)

*Lamp: gardens of the Chi Lin Nunnery*

Nearly every Hong Kong visitor passes through **Central**, whether for sightseeing, taking care of business or en route to Lan Kwai Fong's bars and restaurants. Central also has some impressive architecture: historical remnants, skyscrapers, churches, parks and gardens blend ancient and modern themes. The Star Ferry terminal is a good place to start exploring. It's also the only place to get a glimpse of the city's last surviving rickshaws. West of the terminal, **Exchange Square** (p. 35) is the heart of Hong Kong's business community. See page 45 for a Central amble.

Just uphill from the heart of Central, **Lan Kwai Fong** is a densely packed, pedestrian-only cluster of raucous bars and restaurants. At lunchtime during the week the district becomes a swirling mass of *Chuppies* (Chinese yuppies) trying to squeeze a decent meal into a pitifully short lunch break.

**Sheung Wan**, just west of Central, once had the feel of old Shanghai. The comparison is a bit forced now, since much of the old district has disappeared under the jackhammers of development but there are still tight-

*Soho is alive to the pleasures of café society*

knit communities and shops that carry on business the same way they've done for decades. See page 46 for a neighbourhood walk.

**Soho** (SOuth of HOllywood Rd) is notable for its crush of restaurants. It's a lively place with galleries, *dai pai dongs* (open-air street stalls), antique stores, butchers and a nunnery. The restaurants (pp. 75-6) are strung along Staunton and Elgin Sts west of the escalator.

**Stanley** (meaning 'Red Pillar') is the trendy, suburban *gwailo* (foreigner) place to live. It's on the southeast side of the island, just 15km from Central as the crow flies. There are some great restaurants (p. 80), the famous Stanley Market (p. 40) and a decent beach. See page 49 for an excursion to Stanley.

East of Central, **Wan Chai** (meaning 'Little Bay') is one of Hong Kong's most famous enclaves. A seedy red-light district during the Vietnam War, Wan Chai remains an interesting place to explore. The area between Hennessy and Gloucester Rds has become a major entertainment district. Most of the hybrid bars, restaurants and clubs are clustered along Jaffe and Lockhart Rds, just west of the MTR station.

## Kowloon

The area known as **Kowloon**, which stretches north from Tsim Sha Tsui, once ended in Mong Kok, but the area's glittering malls and neon hotels continue to spread north. This is where Hong Kong and China converge, culturally at least. East doesn't really meet West here, it swallows it up. Kowloon's

*Wan Chai offers more dubious pleasures*

districts are best seen on foot. There aren't too many fantastic sights; it's the overall experience that's worth taking in.

**Mong Kok** has one of the highest population densities of any place in the world, a point that hits home as soon as you arrive. Aside from housing a ridiculous number of people in shabby apartment blocks, Mong Kok is also one of Hong Kong's busiest shopping districts: the name in Cantonese aptly means 'Prosperous Corner'. Locals come to Mong Kok to buy everyday items, but in the streets west of Nathan Rd you'll find many of the city's brothels, revealing Hong Kong's seamier side. See page 47 for a self-guided walk around the area.

*Sensory overload on Mong Kok's Nathan Rd*

Perched at the very edge of the peninsula, **Tsim Sha Tsui** (pronounced jim sa joy) is Hong Kong's tourist ghetto. Countless clothing and shoe stores, restaurants, pubs, sleazy bars, camera and electronics stores and hotels are somehow crammed into a very small area. Around Ashley, Hankow and Lock Rds is a warren of cheap (and often shady) shops, restaurants and bars. It's a fun area to wander around, particularly in the evening.

**Tsim Sha Tsui East**, the triangular block of land east of Chatham Rd, didn't even exist until 1980. Built entirely on reclaimed land, it's a cluster of shopping malls, hotels, restaurants and nightclubs. The new Hong Kong Museum of History (p. 18) is here, right next to the Hong Kong Science Museum (p. 38). Everything is new – there are none of the old, crumbling buildings of nearby Tsim Sha Tsui.

Immediately north of Tsim Sha Tsui – and indistinguishable from it – is **Yau Ma Tei** (pronounced yow ma day). Yau Ma Tei means 'Place of Sesame Plants'. Today the only plants you'll find in this heavily urban district are in the window boxes of crumbling tenements. Yau Ma Tei's narrow byways are good places to check out Hong Kong's

*Serious shopping in Times Square*

more traditional urban society. Within the square bordered by Kansu, Woo Sung, Nanking and Ferry Sts you'll stumble across pawnshops, outdoor markets, Chinese pharmacies, mah jong parlours and other retailers plying their time-honoured trades.

# MUSEUMS

## Flagstaff House Museum of Teaware

(4, F8) The oldest Western-style building still standing in Hong Kong (1846) houses a Chinese teaware collection. Pieces date from the Warring States period (475-221 BC) to the present. There are some rare Chinese ceramics and seals, and interactive exhibits to occupy the kiddies.
✉ Hong Kong Park (off Cotton Tree Dr), Central ☎ 2869 0690 🚇 Admiralty ⏱ Wed-Mon 10am-5pm ⑤ free

## Hong Kong Heritage Museum (1, D7)

Housed in a mock-traditional building, this museum has magnificent displays on Cantonese opera, a children's gallery with toys on show and a gallery for the impressive art collection of Dr TT Tsui. Thematic galleries showcase anything from comics to woodblocks.
✉ 1 Man Lam Rd, Sha Tin ☎ 2180 8188 🖥 www.heritage museum.gov.hk 🚆 Sha Tin KCR (then 10min walk along Tai Po Rd and south along Lion Rock Tunnel Rd). Free shuttle bus Sat, Sun & public holidays

⏱ Wed-Mon 10am-6pm ⑤ $10/5 (free Wed) ♿ excellent

## Hong Kong Museum of Art (3, K5)

The Museum of Art does a good job with classical Chinese art, showcasing paintings and lithographs of old Hong Kong, and a Xubaizhi collection of painting and calligraphy. There are creditable international exhibitions, but the gallery falls down in contemporary art – visit the smaller galleries around for recent Chinese art. Take a break in the hallway and enjoy the harbour views.
✉ 10 Salisbury Rd, Tsim Sha Tsui ☎ 2721 0116 🚇 Tsim Sha Tsui ⏱ Fri-Wed 10am-6pm ⑤ $10/5 (free Wed)

## Hong Kong Museum of Coastal Defence

(2, C4) The history of Hong Kong's coastal defence is presented in the recently restored 300-year-old Lei Yue Mun Fort. Exhibitions in the old Redoubt cover the Ming and Qing dynasties, the colonial years, the Japanese invasion and the resumption of Chinese sovereignty. There's a historical trail through

casements, tunnels and observation posts.
✉ 175 Tung Hei Rd, Shau Kei Wan ☎ 2569 1500 🚇 Shau Kei Wan (then 15min walk north from exit B2), Heng Fa Chuen (then free shuttle bus Sat, Sun & public holidays)
🚌 84, 85, A12 ⏱ Fri-Wed 10am-5pm ⑤ $10/5 (free Wed)

## Law Uk Folk Museum (2, C4)

Small and somewhat shabby, Law Uk has a high quotient of puppetry displays. The house on the grounds is a restored Hakka residence with simple but charming furniture and household items.
✉ 14 Kut Shing St, Chai Wan ☎ 2896 7006 🚇 Chai Wan (then 5min walk west from exit E) ⏱ Tues, Wed, Fri & Sat 10am-1pm & 2-6pm, Sun 1-6pm ⑤ free

## University Museum & Art Gallery (2, C2)

This museum houses ceramics, bronzes, paintings and carvings. Exhibits range from mirrors of the Warring States period through to modern abstracts. There's an intriguing display of crosses made by Nestorians, a Christian sect that arose in Syria and ventured to China probably during the Tang dynasty.
✉ Hong Kong University, 94 Bonham Rd, Western/Kennedy Town ☎ 2241 5500 🖥 www.hku.hk/hkumag 🚌 3B, 23, 40 ⏱ Mon-Sat 9.30am-6pm, Sun 1.30-5.30pm ⑤ free

*Take time to discover Hong Kong at its museums*

# BUILDINGS & PLACES OF WORSHIP

### Chi Lin Nunnery
(2, A3) This Tang-style wooden complex is a serene place with lotus ponds, immaculate bonsai and silent nuns delivering offerings of fruit and rice to Buddha and deities. Built in 1998 using ancient techniques, the design is intended to show the harmony of humans with nature – it's convincing until you look up at the looming high-rises nearby.
✉ **5 Chi Lin Dr, Diamond Hill ☎ 2354 1882 ⊕ Diamond Hill (then 5min walk along Fung Tak from exit C2) ⏲ Thurs-Tues 9am-4pm ⑤ free**

### Clock Tower (3, K3)
This 45m clock tower, built in 1922, is all that remains of the southern terminus of the Kowloon-Canton Railway (built in 1916 and torn down in 1978). The original building, which had columns and was colonial in style, was too small to handle the large volume of passenger traffic. You can climb the steps of the tower for an impeded view every Sunday from 10am to 6pm.
✉ **sth of Salisbury Rd, Tsim Sha Tsui ⊕ Tsim Sha Tsui ⏲ tours Sun 10am-6pm ⑤ free**

### Exchange Square
(4, D6) Elevated above the fray, the square is the seat of the Hong Kong Stock Exchange. The huge statue in front of the Forum Mall is of a taijiquan posture known as 'snake creeps down'. Ground level gives over to the bus station.
✉ **cnr Connaught Rd Central & Pedder St, Central ⊕ Central ⑤ free**

### Former Government House (4, F5)
The governor's ex-residence dates back to 1858, though its tower was added by the Japanese during WWII. The current chief executive, Tung Chee Hwa, turned down the offer to make it his abode, saying the *fung shui* wasn't satisfactory.
✉ **Upper Albert Rd, Central ⊕ Central ⏲ open one Sun in Mar**

### Hong Kong Convention & Exhibition Centre
(4, D12) This enormous complex boasts the world's

*The glass curtain at the Convention & Exhibition Centre*

largest 'glass curtain', a window seven storeys high. Expanded onto reclaimed land for the handover ceremony in June 1997, the extension reaches out into the harbour. The design of the extension is spectacular, symbolising a bird in flight (pop over to the Sky Lobby in Central Plaza for an overview).
✉ **1 Expo Dr, Wan Chai ☎ 2582 8888 ⓔ www.hkcec.com.hk ⊕ Wan Chai 🚊 yes 🚌 10A, 20, 21 ⏲ 9am-7pm (variable) ⑤ free (charges for some exhibitions) ♿ good**

## Tallest Building?
The International Finance Centre's new tower (IFC 2; 4, C6) was being built at the time of writing. Once completed it will reach 88 storeys high and increase the IFC space to 1.56 million sq m: pretty massive in a city where office rent goes for $75,000/sq m.

### Hong Kong Cultural Centre (3, K4)

The Cultural Centre is one of Hong Kong's great landmarks. Within the skin-coloured tiled exterior there's a 2100-seat concert hall, theatres, rehearsal studios, an arts library and an impressive main lobby. There are daily tours from 12.30pm to 1pm.

✉ cnr Salisbury & Canton Rds, Tsim Sha Tsui ☎ 2734 2009 ⊕ Tsim Sha Tsui ⊘ Mon-Sat 9am-11pm, Sun 1-11pm ⑤ free; tours $10/5 ♿ good

### Hongkong & Shanghai Bank Building (4, F6)

This 180m-tall glass and aluminium building is an innovative masterpiece. Locals call it the 'Robot Building', as you can see the chains and motors of the escalators and other moving parts whirring away inside. Structurally, the building is equally radical, built on a 'coat-hanger' frame. Stand in the atrium and look up to see how the structure hangs, rather than ascends.

✉ 1 Queen's Rd, Central ⊕ Central ⑤ free; tours $10/5 ⓘ 1st fl information counter ♿ good

### Jardine House (4, D6)

This 40-storey silver monolith is the HQ of Hong Kong's venerable conglomerate, Jardine Matheson. The building's porthole-style windows have earned it a less respectable Chinese nickname, which translates as 'Thousand Arseholes'. To the east of the building is Henry Moore's sculpture *Double Oval*.

✉ cnr Connaught Rd Central & Pedder St, Central ⊕ Central ⊘ Mon-Sat 7am-9pm ⑤ free ♿ fair

### Kowloon Mosque & Islamic Centre (3, G4)

The present mosque (Hong Kong's largest) was completed in 1984 and occupies the site of a previous mosque (built in 1896) for Muslim Indian troops who were garrisoned in barracks at what is now Kowloon Park. The mosque, with its handsome dome, minarets and carved marble, is interesting to admire from the outside. Muslims are welcome to attend services but non-Muslims should ask if it's OK to look inside – remember to take off your shoes.

✉ 105 Nathan Rd, Tsim Sha Tsui ☎ 2724 0095 ⊕ Tsim Sha Tsui

*A founding father*

### Legislative Council Building (4, E6)

This colonnaded neoclassical building is the old Supreme Court. Out the front is a blind-folded statue of the Greek goddess Themis, who represents justice.

✉ Jackson Rd, Central ⊕ Central 🚇 yes ⑤ free ♿ fair

### Lei Cheng Uk Museum & Han Tomb (2, B2)

This Eastern Han dynasty (AD 25-220) burial vault was discovered in 1955 when workers were levelling the hillside for a housing estate. The tomb is encased in a concrete shell for protection and you can only peek through a plastic window.

✉ Lei Cheng Uk Estate, 41 Tonkin St, Cheung Sha Wan ☎ 2386 2863 ⊕ Cheung Sha Wan (then 10min walk up Tonkin St from exit A3) 🚌 2 ⊘ Mon-Wed, Fri & Sat 10am-1pm & 2-6pm, Sun 1-6pm ⑤ free

### Lippo Centre (4, F8)

These twin towers epitomise the brash 1980s: one glance at the 'sky rooms' (lumpy protrusions) and you know you're in

*No, it's not Stonehenge: Hong Kong Cultural Centre*

shoulder-pad land. Although weather-beaten, the building still stands out for its adventurous design.
✉ **89 Queensway, Admiralty** Ⓜ **Admiralty** 🚇 **yes** Ⓢ **free** ♿ **fair**

### St John's Cathedral

**(4, F6)** Built in 1847, this Anglican church is now lost in Central's forest of skyscrapers. Between 1942 and 1944 the Japanese Imperial Army used it as a social club and the building was ravaged. The wooden front doors were rebuilt after the war using timber salvaged from HMS *Tamar*, a British warship that guarded the entrance to Victoria Harbour. Behind the cathedral is the 1917 French Mission building, now home to Hong Kong's Court of Final Appeal.
✉ **4-8 Garden Rd, Central** ☎ **2523 4157** Ⓜ **Central** ⏱ **7am-6pm (plus daily services)**

### The Centre

**(6, A4)** This star-shaped building will have you staring for a few reasons. From close up, the protruding corners of the building can appear to cut into the structure. But what really sets it apart is the awesome nightly light show that sends colour lights cascading down the towering spines. It's also home to the Hong Kong Tourism Board (HKTB).
✉ **99 Queens Rd, Central** Ⓜ **Central** 🚇 **yes** Ⓢ **free** ♿ **excellent**

### Tin Hau Temple, Tin Hau

**(1, G5)** Just east of Victoria Park, this tiny temple dedicated to Tin Hau, the goddess of

*The striking, prismatic flanks of the Lippo Centre*

seafarers, is dwarfed by surrounding high-rises. Before reclamation, the temple stood on the waterfront. This has been a site of worship for 300 years, though the current structure is only about 200 years old.
✉ **10 Tin Hau Temple Rd (at Dragon Rd)** Ⓜ **Tin Hau** ⏱ **8am-6pm**

### Tin Hau Temple, Yau Ma Tei

**(3, A4)** A few blocks northeast of the Jade Market, this other Tin Hau temple is quite sizable. The temple complex also houses an altar dedicated to Shing Wong (god of the city) and To Tei (god of the Earth).
✉ **off Nathan Rd (btw Market & Public Sq Sts)** Ⓜ **Yau Ma Tei** ⏱ **8am-6pm**

### Wong Tai Sin Temple

**(2, A3)** This large, active Taoist temple was built in 1973. Like most Chinese temples, this one is an explosion of colour. Come in the early evening and watch hordes of devotees praying and divining the future with fortune sticks. Adjacent to the temple is

an arcade populated by fortune tellers, some of whom speak good English. Behind the main temple are the Good Wish Gardens, replete with colourful pavilions, curved pathways and an artificial waterway.
✉ **adjacent Wong Tai Sin MTR, Wong Tai Sin** Ⓜ **Wong Tai Sin** ⏱ **7am-6pm**

### Sage Sticks

In the late afternoon and early evening Wong Tai Sin Temple is always abuzz with people praying and divining the future with *chim* (fortune sticks). The temple is flanked by stacks of these sticks housed in bamboo canisters, which people hold, ask the spirits or gods a question then shake the canister until one stick falls out. Each stick bears a numeral, which corresponds to a printed slip of paper in a set held by the temple keeper. That slip of paper is taken to the temple's fortune-teller, who interprets its meaning.

# HONG KONG FOR CHILDREN

The upside about bringing children to Hong Kong is that people are tolerant of child-caused chaos. Or, more accurately, restaurants and shopping centres are usually so noisy that no-one will blink if a toddler throws a tantrum. There are playgrounds dotted around but there aren't many public parks where you can let the wild things exhaust themselves. That said, the colour and vibrancy of Hong Kong's sights will appeal to children.

## More Kiddie Attractions

**Big Wave Bay** (p. 51) Shek O's waves aren't big, there's a playground, shops and no cars  **Dim Sum Meals** (p. 71) a loud, lucky-dip lunch  **Hong Kong Heritage Museum** (p. 34) interactive display paradise  **Hong Kong Park** (p. 27) birds, waterfalls and playgrounds  **Mong Kok Mooch** (p. 47) stimulating streetscape taking in **Yuen Po St Bird Garden** (p. 42)  **Public Transport** (p. 110-11) from the space-age MTR to the rattling trams  **Repulse Bay** (p. 28) beach and Buddhist statues  **Star & Inter-Island Ferries** (p. 19) boat-bumping brilliance  **Tsim Sha Tsui Promenade** (p. 15) a light show every night  **Wong Tai Sin Temple** (p. 37) prayers, pagodas and pungent incense  **Zoological & Botanic Gardens** (p. 41) animal overload

## Hong Kong Science Museum (3, F7)

The Science Museum is a multilevel complex with more than 500 displays on computers, energy, physics, robotics, telecommunications, health and much more. Most exhibits are 'hands on', which helps to keep younger visitors interested. All in all it's a great place for kids of all ages and not a bad place for grown-ups either, who will probably realise how interesting science classes could have been.

✉ 2 Science Museum Rd, Tsim Sha Tsui East
☎ 2732 3232
⊕ Tsim Sha Tsui
🚌 5C, 8
⊙ Tues-Fri 1-9pm, Sat-Sun 10am-9pm
$ $25/12.50 ♿ good

## Hong Kong Space Museum & Theatre

(3, J4) This golf ball–shaped building is divided into the Hall of Space Science, the Hall of Astronomy and the Space Theatre planetarium. Exhibits include a lump of moon rock, rocket-ship models and NASA's 1962 *Mercury* space capsule. The Space Theatre screens 'sky shows' and IMAX films in English and Cantonese.

✉ 10 Salisbury Rd, Tsim Sha Tsui ☎ 2734 2722 ⊕ Tsim Sha Tsui
⊙ museum: Mon, Wed & Fri 1-9pm, Sat-Sun 10am-9pm; theatre: Tues-Sun 12.30-8.30pm
$ museum $10/5; theatre shows from $32/16
♿ excellent

## Ocean Park (2, D3)

Ocean Park, near Aberdeen, is an amusement park replete with stomach-turning rides. It is also a marine park, with dolphin and killer-whale shows and a reef aquarium. The two-part complex is linked by a scenic cable-car ride. The park entrance is on the 'lowland' side and the main section is on the 'headlands' and affords views of the South China Sea. At the rear is the Middle Kingdom Chinese cultural village: a whitewashed version of ancient China.

☎ 2552 0291 🌐 www.oceanpark.com.hk
🚌 Ocean Park Citybus from Admiralty or Central Star Ferry terminal ⊙ Sun-Fri 10am-6pm, Sat 10am-11pm
$ $180/90 ♿ excellent

## Babysitting & Childcare

Most hotels will be able to recommend a babysitter if you've got daytime appointments or want a night out *sans* child. Otherwise call Rent-A-Mum (☎ 2523 4868; 🌐 rentamum@hknet.com), a reputable agency that supplies qualified English-speaking nannies for $95/hr.

Pan Bookshop
158-162 Fulham Road
London

SW10 9PG

TEL:020 7373 4997
VAT NO:VAT REG 199440621

11-10-03   12:12   SALE   2 2760
ASSISTANT

| PRODUCT | QTY | Amt | VAT |
|---|---|---|---|
| Lonely Planet: Hong Kon | 1 | 6.99 | Z |

| ZERO RATE | 6.99 | 6.99 |
|---|---|---|
| TOTAL | 1 | 6.99 |
| CASH | | 10.00 |
| TOTAL TENDERED | | 10.00 |
| CHANGE | | 3.01 |

THANK YOU FOR YOUR CUSTOM
PLEASE CALL AGAIN....

# GALLERIES

Many of the galleries are in the Soho area (Map 6), making it perfect for a mid-afternoon art-crawl. As well as galleries listed, check out these Central/Soho galleries: **Fringe Club** (6, E5) 2 Lwr Albert Rd; **10 Chancery Lane Gallery** (6, D3); **Plum Blossoms** (6, C3) 1 Hollywood Rd; **Schoeni Art Gallery** (6, D2; 6, C3) 21-31 Old Bailey St & 27 Hollywood Rd; and **Agnes B** (6, C2) 22 Elgin St.

## Cattle Depot Artist Village (2, B3)

Kowloon's slaughterhouse has changed its focus from abattoir to artistry. The beautiful red-brick buildings were saved from the demolition ball and are home to local artists who live, work and exhibit within the depot. It's pot-luck but there's always something showing, making it a great space to explore that's off the beaten track.
✉ 63 Ma Tau Kok Rd, Kowloon ☎ 2104 3322
🚍 106, 3B, 5C, 5D, 11B, 21, 11K, 12A, 61X, 85A, 85C ⏰ Tues-Sun 2-8pm ⑤ free ♿ fair

## Galerie Martini (6, D5)

Small upstairs art nook that shows international contemporary art. The exhibitions swing between relatively established Western artists and local artists on the rise.
✉ 1st fl, 99f Wellington St, Soho ☎ 2526 9566
🌐 www.galeriemartini .com 🚇 Central
⏰ Tues-Sat 11am-7pm ⑤ free ♿ fair

## HanArt TZ Gallery (4, F6)

One of the most influential and innovative galleries in Hong Kong showing contemporary Chinese art with a thoroughbred stable of figurative and conceptual painters, sculptors and

*Plum Blossoms gallery*

video artists.
✉ Henley Bldg, 5 Queen's Rd Central, Central ☎ 2526 9019
🚇 Central 🅿 yes
⏰ Mon-Sat 10am-6.30pm ⑤ free ♿ fair

## John Batten Gallery (6, C1)

Small gallery charged with the enthusiasm and vision of its namesake director. Batten shows local and international painting, photography and video art of consistently high quality.
✉ 64 Peel St, Soho
☎ 2854 1018
🚇 Central ⏰ Tues-Sat 11am-7pm, Sun 1-5pm ⑤ free

## Pao Galleries (4, F11)

Major contemporary art gallery in the Hong Kong Arts Centre. Extending over floors 4 and 5, there's room to host retrospectives and group shows in all visual media. The curatorial vision is lively without being too provocative.
✉ 2 Harbour Rd, Wan Chai ☎ 2582 0200
🚇 Wan Chai
⏰ 10am-8pm ⑤ free

## Para/Site Art Space (4, C1)

Adventurous, artist-run art space that knows no boundaries when it comes to mixing media. Most art on display is Chinese but there are occasional exhibitions by European and Australian artists. There's a small yet finger-on-pulse collection of books for sale.
✉ 2 Po Yan St, Sheung Wan ☎ 2517 4620
🌐 www.para-site.org.hk
🚇 Sheung Wan
⏰ Wed-Sun noon-7pm ⑤ free

## Shanghai St Artspace Exhibition Hall (2, B2)

Run by the Hong Kong Arts Development Council, this small space in a strange location concentrates on local modern art. Video assemblages, photography, computer art and mixed media all get a look-in.
✉ 404 Shanghai St, Yau Ma Tei (p. 47) ☎ 2770 2157 🚇 Yau Ma Tei
⏰ Thurs-Tues 10.30am-7.30pm ⑤ free

# MARKETS

## Cat St Market (4, C2)

Lascar Row is the official name of this pedestrian-only laneway lined with antique and curio shops and stalls selling found objects, cheap jewellery, ornaments, carvings and newly minted ancient coins. Cat St is a fun place to prowl around for a trinket or two.

✉ Lascar Row, Sheung Wan ⊖ Sheung Wan ⊙ noon-10pm

## Jade Market (3, B3)

This market comprises a couple of hundred stalls selling all varieties and grades of jade from inside a large tent. Unless you really know your jade, it's probably not wise to buy any expensive pieces here.

✉ Kansu St, near Gascoigne Rd overpass, Yau Ma Tei ⊖ Jordan, Yau Ma Tei 🚌 9 ⊙ 10am-3.30pm ♿ good

## Li Yuen St (6, B5)

Actually two streets,

Kowloon has markets as Chinese as any over the border

Li Yuen St E and Li Yuen St W run parallel to each other between Des Voeux and Queen's Rds, opposite the Lane Crawford department store. Closed to motorised traffic, the lanes are crammed with shops selling clothing, fabrics and assorted knick-knacks.

✉ Li Yuen Sts E & W, Central ⊖ Central 🚋 yes

## Stanley Market (2, E4)

No big bargains, no big stings, just reasonably priced casual clothes (plenty of large sizes), knick-knacks, toys and formulaic art, all in a nicely confusing maze of alleys near the foreshore. It's not worth a trip in itself but combined with a meal and a wander around Stanley, the market makes for a great day trip.

🚌 6, 66, 262 (from Exchange Sq) ⊙ Mon-Fri 10am-5.30pm, Sat-Sun 10am-7pm 🅢 free ♿ good

## Tung Choi St (Ladies') Market

(2, B2) The Tung Choi St

market is a cheek to jowl affair, offering up cheap clothes and trinkets. People start setting up their stalls as early as noon, but it's better to get here after 6pm when there's much more on offer.

✉ Tung Choi St (btw Dundas & Argyle Sts), Mong Kok (p. 47) ⊖ Mong Kok ⊙ 6pm-midnight

## Western Market

(4, B2) Opposite Central's Macau ferry terminal, this four-storey Edwardian building, built in 1906, was reopened in 1991 as a shopping centre. It's filled to the brim with modern shops selling a huge range of small antiques, embroideries and collectibles (Hello Kitty freaks are sure in for a treat). The 1st floor is a 'cloth alley', similar to Hong Kong's fast-disappearing outdoor markets. Some good silks can also be bought here.

✉ Connaught Rd W (cnr Chung Kong Rd), Sheung Wan ⊖ Sheung Wan 🚋 yes ⊙ 10am-7pm

---

### Hong Kong Horticulture

The flower on Hong Kong's flag is the *Bauhinia Blakeana,* or Hong Kong Orchid Tree. From November to March you may see the fragrant, purple Bauhinia blooming in **Victoria Park** (p. 42), **Kowloon Walled City Park** (p. 41) or on Mong Kok's aptly named **Flower Market Rd** (p. 47).

# PARKS, GARDENS & PUBLIC SPACES

### Hong Kong Zoological & Botanic Gardens (4, G5)

These excellent gardens, established in 1864, are a pleasant collection of fountains, sculptures, greenhouses, aviaries, a zoo and a playground. There are hundreds of species of birds, exotic trees, plants and shrubs on display. The animal displays seem to be mostly primates; other residents include a lone jaguar. Don't come if you find small concrete cages upsetting. The gardens are divided by Albany Rd, with the plants and aviaries in one area, off Garden Rd, and most of the animals in the other.

✉ **Albany Rd, Central**
☎ **2530 0154**
🚇 Central 🚌 3B, 12, 12A, 12M ⏰ 6am-10pm; zoo: 6am-7pm; greenhouse: 9am-4.30pm ⑤ free ♿ fair

### Kowloon Park (3, F3)

Once the site of the Whitfield Barracks for British and Indian troops, this area has been reborn as an oasis of green and a refreshing escape from the clutter and bustle of Nathan Rd. Pathways and walls crisscross the grass,

*Hong Kong's parkland is well worth exploring*

birds hop around in cages, and towers and viewpoints dot the landscape. The Sculpture Walk features works by local artists. There's an excellent indoor/outdoor pool complex complete with waterfalls. If you wish to swim, go on a weekday morning or afternoon; on weekends there are so many bathers it's tough to even see the water.

✉ **Tsim Sha Tsui**
☎ **2724 4100** 🚇 Tsim Sha Tsui, Jordan ⏰ 6am-midnight; pools: Apr-Oct ⑤ free

### Kowloon Walled City Park (2, A3)

The walls that enclose this beautiful park were once the perimeter of a notorious village that technically remained part of China throughout British rule. The enclave was known for its vice, prostitution, gambling and, worst of all, illegal dentists. In 1984 the Hong Kong government acquired the area, evicted the residents and replaced them with pavilions, ponds, turtles, goldfish and exquisite flora, including a long

hedge coaxed into the form of a dragon. The park opened in 1996.

✉ **cnr Tung Tau Tsuen & Tung Tsing Rds, Kowloon City** 🚇 Lok Fu (then taxi or 15min walk along Junction & Tung Tau Tsuen Rds) 🚌 1 ⏰ 6.30am-10pm ⑤ free ♿ good

### Statue Square (4, E6)

Statue Square once displayed effigies of England's royalty. The statues were taken down by the Japanese during WWII. Fittingly, the sole

## Sculpture Sanctuary

If you can't face another moment of Nathan Rd's roaring buses and touting tailors, take time out betwixt the artwork in Kowloon Park's Sculpture Walk. Dotted among the greenery are about 30 marble, bronze and other weather-hardy sculptures by both local and overseas artists.

*Taking five: Victoria Park*

*Get in touch with nature at Hong Kong Park's aviary*

survivor is a bronze likeness of Sir Thomas Jackson, a particularly successful Victorian-era head of the Hongkong & Shanghai Bank. On the northern side of Chater Rd is the cenotaph dedicated to Hong Kong residents who died in WWI and WWII.

✉ **Chater Rd, Central** ⊖ **Central** 🚊 **yes**

## Maid in Hong Kong

On Sundays, Hong Kong's Filipino maids take over the pavements and public squares of Central. They come in their hundreds to share food, gossip, play cards and do one another's hair. You can't miss them around Statue Square (they call the statue of Jackson 'the black man'). There are about 140,000 Filipino maids in Hong Kong, most on two-year visas. The city's 60,000 Indonesian maids converge on Victoria Park every Sunday for picnics and impromptu soccer matches.

**Victoria Park** (5, E4)
One of the biggest patches of green grass on the northern side of Hong Kong Island, Victoria Park is also one of the territory's most popular escapes. The best time to stroll around is during daylight hours Monday to Friday. Early in the morning this is an excellent place to watch the slow-motion choreography of practitioners of taijiquan, and there's a pebble garden to stroll over and massage your soles. Between April and October you can take a dip in the swimming pool. The park becomes a flower market a few days before the Chinese New Year. It's also worth a visit

during the Mid-Autumn (Moon) Festival.
✉ east of Causeway Bay ⊖ Causeway Bay 🚊 yes

**Yuen Po St Bird Garden** (2, B2)
There are hundreds of birds for sale here along with elaborate cages carved from teak and bamboo. The best bamboo cages are repeatedly soaked, softened and dried as they are shaped, sometimes up to 10 times. The Chinese have long favoured birds as pets, especially those that can sing. In fact a bird's singing prowess often determines its price. Some birds are also considered harbingers of good fortune, which is why they are sometimes taken to horse races. The birds seem to live pretty well: the owners use chopsticks to feed live grasshoppers to their singing feathered friends, and give them honey nectar to gild their vocal cords.
✉ btw Boundary St & Flower Market Rd, Yau Ma Tei (p. 47) ⊖ Prince Edward 🚌 1, 1A 🚉 Mong Kok KCR ⏰ 8am-7pm 💲 free ♿ fair

*Foot massage: Victoria Park pebble garden*

# QUIRKY HONG KONG

Sure, we've all strapped a kid to a bamboo pole and waved him or her around in a parade. Who of us hasn't made a half-coffee/half-tea cuppa, just for kicks? And of course we all throw oranges high into a tree when we want to give fate a hop along. We just don't do them all on the same day, which is what you can do in Hong Kong.

## Central Market (6, A4)

You shouldn't have any trouble finding this huge Bauhaus-design wholesale market – just sniff the air. It's more a zoo than a market, with everything from chickens and quail to eels and crabs, alive or freshly slaughtered. The squeamish should give it a miss.

✉ btw Des Voeux & Queen's Rds and Jubilee & Queen Victoria Sts, Central
☎ 2869 8802
🚇 Central  🚻 yes
🕐 5am-noon

## Central–Mid-Levels Escalator (6, A4-E1)

The world's longest covered outdoor people mover is part commuter travelator, part sightseeing ride and part pick-up procession. It consists of elevated escalators, moving walkways and linking stairs covering the 800m hill from Central's offices to the Mid-Levels' apartments. The funniest bit is past the Shelley St bars – travelators have just enough time to flirt with barflies as they glide by.

✉ Cochrane, Shelley & Peel Sts  🚇 Central
🕐 downhill 6-10am; uphill 10.20am-midnight  💲 free

## Cheung Chau Bun Festival (1, G4)

The Bun Festival of Tai Chiu takes place in May and is famous for its bun towers – bamboo scaffolding

---

### Act Normal, Do Strange

If you want to have a day you can *really* tell your friends about, do like this:

- breakfast on pig organ congee at Happy Garden Noodle & Congee Kitchen (p. 81)
- buy some party-bondage gear at Onitsuka (p. 59)
- walk over the Longevity Bridge at Repulse Bay (p. 28)
- have a *yuan yang* (half-coffee/half-tea) at Dai Pai Dong (p. 72)
- buy and try a durian at the Central Market (p. 43)
- stock up on lily bulbs at Eu Yan Sang (p. 67)

---

standing up to 20m high and covered with holy bread buns. On the 3rd day of the festival (a Sunday) there's a lively procession with stilt walkers and colourfully dressed 'floating children' who are carried through the streets strapped to long waving poles.

✉ Pak Tai Temple, Pak She St, Cheung Chau
⛴ Cheung Chau (from Central)  💲 free

## Noonday Gun (5, E3)

One of the few vestiges of Causeway Bay's colonial past is this 3lb cannon built by Hotchkiss of Portsmouth in 1901. It stands in front of the Excelsior Hotel (accessible via a tunnel under the road from the World Trade Centre basement) and is fired daily at noon. Exactly how this tradition started is not known. Noel Coward made the gun famous with his satirical 1924 song 'Mad Dogs and

Englishmen', about colonists who braved the heat of the noonday sun while the locals stayed indoors: *'In Hong Kong they strike a gong/and fire off a noonday gun/to reprimand each inmate/who's in late.'*

✉ 281 Gloucester Rd, Causeway Bay
🚇 Causeway Bay

## Wishing Tree (1, C6)

If you're crossing your fingers and avoiding the cracks but still haven't got lucky, pay a visit to the wishing tree. This large banyan beauty is laden with wishes written on swatches of paper tied to oranges. You write your wish on the fruit and then throw it as high as you can into the tree. The higher it goes, the more chance there is of your wish coming true.

✉ Lam Tsuen, Lam Kam Rd, Tai Po  🚉 Tai Po KCR (then bus 64K)
💲 free

# KEEPING FIT

Walking and taijiquan are the most popular physical activities in Hong Kong. Golf is a rich person's sport, undertaken more for networking and prestige rather than fitness. Tennis and gym sessions are also popular, and most top-end hotels have gyms and pools. Both Kowloon Park (p. 41) and Victoria Park (p. 42) have swimming pools that are more for leisure than lapping.

*Um...free memberships?*

### New York Fitness Gym (6, C3)

This well-equipped gym has free weights, resistance training, punch bags and fitness classes. It's right by the Central–Mid-Levels escalator so you can impress passing trade.
✉ **32 Hollywood Rd, Soho** ☎ **2543 2280**
🚇 **Central** ⏰ **Mon-Fri 6.45am-10.30pm, Sat-Sun 7.30am-9pm**
💲 **$500/wk**

*Hoop dreams*

### Discovery Bay Golf Club (1, E4)

This 18-hole course is open to visitors Monday, Tuesday and Friday but you need to book two days in advance.
✉ **Discovery Bay, Lantau** ☎ **2987 7273; bookings 2987 2112**
🚢 **Discovery Bay (from Central)** 💲 **green fees $1400**

### The Jockey Club Kau Sai Chau Public Golf Course (1, D9)

Hong Kong's only public golf course is postcard perfect, with dramatic views west over Sai Kung. Book in for a round, eat at the club restaurant, stay for the day.
✉ **Kau Sai Chau Island, New Territories**
☎ **2791 3388**
📧 **www.kscgolf.com**
🚢 **Sai Kung Harbour ($50 return)** ⏰ **7am-8pm** 💲 **18 holes $540**

### Paradise Ladies Health Club (4, G11)

This gym might suit women who would rather work up a sweat without male company. Also has facials and other beauty treatments.
✉ **20th fl, 23 Thomson Rd, Wan Chai** ☎ **2529 5252** 🚇 **Wan Chai**
⏰ **Mon-Fri 7.30am-10pm, Sat-Sun noon-6pm**

### Victoria Park Tennis Centre (5, D5)

There are 13 tennis courts at this easy-to-find complex near Tin Hau station. Try it during business hours.
✉ **Hing Fat St, Victoria Park, Causeway Bay**
☎ **2570 6186** 🚇 **Tin Hau** ⏰ **7am-10pm**
💲 **day: $42/hr; evening: $57/hr**

## Slow Down, Tune In, Tone Up

- **Healing Plants** (6, C4; ☎ 2815 5005) 17 Lyndhurst Tce, Central – acupuncture, reflexology, Swedish massage and other therapies.
- **Happy Foot Massage** (6, B4; ☎ 2544 1010) 11-13th fl, 98-102 Wellington St, Central – give your major mode of transport a pampering at the aptly named Happy Foot. If you don't you'll kick yourself.
- **Taijiquan Lessons** with the HKTB (p. 55)
- **Yoga Central** (6, D5; ☎ 2982 4308; 📧 www.yogacentral.com.hk) 4th fl, 13 Wyndham St, Lan Kwai Fong – Hatha yoga with an Iyengar spin, this place has beginner and intermediate classes Monday to Saturday (1hr $120); ring ahead to reserve your spot.

# out & about

## WALKING TOURS
### Central Amble

Begin at the Star Ferry terminal ❶ in Central. With your back to the water, take the elevated walkway to the right and follow signs to Exchange Square ❷ and Jardine House ❸. Cross Connaught Place and take the underground walkway through to Chater Rd and Statue Square ❹. Cross the square and head east past the Legislative Council Building ❺ to Chater Garden. Cross Queen's Rd Central and Garden Rd, which brings you to the Bank of China Tower ❻. Head east under the bridge and follow the path to the Flagstaff House Museum of Teaware ❼ in Hong

**distance** 2km **duration** 1hr
► **start** 🚢 Star Ferry Ⓜ Central
● **end** Ⓜ Central

*Snap happy in Hong Kong Park*

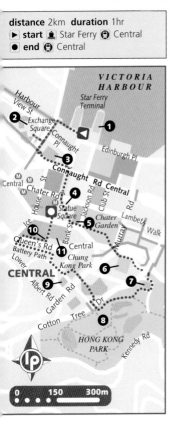

Kong Park ❽. Walkways west over Cotton Tree Dr, through the Citybank Plaza, over Garden Rd and through Chung Kong Park bring you to St John's Cathedral ❾. Take Battery Path down to Queen's Rd, cross over and walk east. If you're hungry, Mix ❿ is a good spot for wraps and juices, and next door is the Hongkong & Shanghai Bank Building ⓫. Walk through the ground-floor plaza: entrance K to Central MTR is accessible from the western side of Statue Square.

## Sheung Wan Shuffle

Browse Des Voeux Rd W's dried seafood shops ❶ then turn up Ko Shing St where there are herbal wholesalers ❷. At the end of the street, walk briefly along Des Voeux Rd and turn right onto Bonham Strand W, which is lined with ginseng sellers ❸. Hook right onto Bonham Strand and up to Queen's Rd W. To the left you'll find shops selling bird's nests (for soup!) and paper funeral offerings for the dead ❹. Across Queen's Rd is Possession St ❺, where Captain Elliot first planted the Union Jack in 1841. Climbing Pound Lane to where it meets Tai Ping Shan St, look to the right to find Pak Sing Temple ❻, built in the 1850s to hold ancestral tablets brought from China. Descend Upper Station St to Hollywood Rd's antique shops ❼. Continuing east on Hollywood Rd brings you to Man Mo Temple ❽. Take a short hop down Ladder St to Upper Lascar Row, home of Cat St Market ❾. Ladder St brings you to Queen's Rd again, which you can cross to Hillier St ❿ for a street-stall snack, or to buy a parrot. On Bonham Strand, head east to Man Wa Lane ⓫ where you can have a traditional chop (seal) made.

### SIGHTS & HIGHLIGHTS

Dried seafood shops
Herbal wholesalers and ginseng sellers
Bird's nests
Possession St
Pak Sing Temple
Antique shops (pp. 66-7)
Man Mo Temple (p. 23)
Cat St Market (p. 40)
Street stalls
Man Wa Lane

*Potions and elixirs: Queen's Rd*

**distance** 1.9km **duration** 1hr
▶ **start** 🚋 Kennedy Town to Sutherland St
● **end** 🚇 Sheung Wan

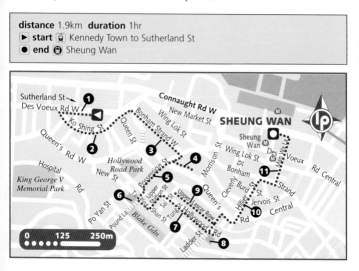

# Mong Kok to Jordan Mooch

Take exit A from Prince Edward MTR, walk north up Nathan Rd, then turn right onto Boundary St. The Yuen Po St Bird Garden ❶ is a 10min walk away. Continue out the back to Flower Market Rd ❷ where there are thousands of lovely blooms to behold. At the end of the street, turn left onto Sai Yee St, then right onto Prince Edward Rd W. At Tung Choi St turn left: the first couple of blocks are dominated by bright goldfish shops ❸. South of Argyle St, the Ladies' Market ❹ takes over. Turn right at Dundas St – the Trendy Zone mall ❺ is on the corner of Nathan Rd. Cross over and turn left into Shanghai St

**distance** 4.5km  **duration** 2hrs
▶ **start** Ⓜ Prince Edward
● **end** Ⓜ Jordan

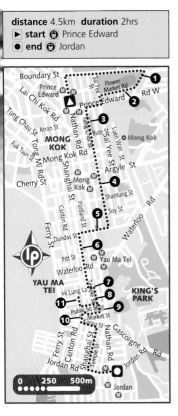

where you'll find the Shanghai St Artspace Exhibition Hall ❻ at No 404 and a woodcarving shop at No 342. Cut down Hi Lung Lane to Temple St where you can choose a cheap lunch ❼. The Temple St Night Market ❽ runs right down to Jordan Rd, separated by Tin Hau Temple ❾ and the Jade Market ❿. If you want to rest, see what's showing at Broadway Cinematheque ⓫; there's a café here too.

## Night Light

Festive they may be, but those pink and green neon arrows strung along Mong Kok's streets are code for brothels. You'll also see a lot of 'hourly' hotels. Though Mong Kok is a pretty seedy part of town, there's no appreciable rise in street crime to go along with it.

## Cheung Chau Canter

Disembark the ferry and turn left past Praya St's restaurants into Pak She Praya Rd, from where you'll see houseboats in the harbour. Take Pak She Fourth Lane to Pak Tai Temple ❶, site of the colourful Bun Festival held in May. Head south along Pak She St and dogleg into San Hing St past shops selling paper offerings, herbs and incense. Turn left at Tung Wan Rd – the Garden Café ❷ at No 84 has good Western food. The beach ❸ at the end of the street is popular with windsurfers and swimmers. Walk south along the shore to the Warwick Hotel ❹. At the front are some rock carvings from 500 BC. Return and head up Cheung Chau Sports Rd (behind the hotel), then right onto Kwun Yum Wan Rd. Pass the sports ground and soon you'll come to Kwan Kung Pavilion ❺, dedicated to Kwan Tai, god of war and righteousness. A left turn out of the temple puts you on Peak Rd, which leads along a scenic ridge, through the cemetery down to the ferry pier at Sai Wan ❻. The view is especially atmospheric at dusk. Either take a boat back to Cheung Chau village (where you began) or take the path to Cheung Po Tsai Cave ❼, an old pirate hang-out. Back at Cheung Chau village, round off your day by relaxing with a plate of freshly cooked seafood on the waterfront.

### SIGHTS & HIGHLIGHTS

Pak Tai Temple (see Cheung Chau Bun
    Festival p. 43)
Garden Café
Tung Wan Beach
Rock Carvings at Warwick Hotel
Kwan Kung Pavilion
Cheung Chau Cemetery
Sai Wan
Cheung Po Tsai Cave

**distance** 4.5km  **duration** 2.5hrs
▶ **start** 🚢 Central–Cheung Chau
● **end** 🚢 Cheung Chau–Central

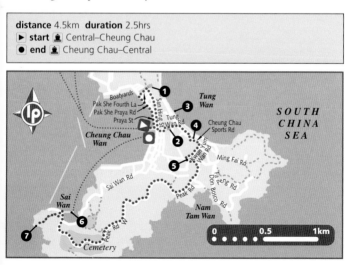

# EXCURSIONS

## Lamma Island    (2, E1)

The third-largest island, after Lantau and Hong Kong, Lamma is *the* haven for expats. Known mainly for its seafood restaurants, Lamma also has good beaches and hikes.

Walking between the two main townships, **Yung Shue Wan** and **Sok Kwu Wan**, takes just over an hour via popular **Hung Shing Ye Beach**. South of the beach, the path climbs steeply until it reaches a pavilion near the top of the hill.

### INFORMATION

*10km south of Central*

🚇 Central/Aberdeen–Yung Shue Wan/ Sok Kwu Wan

ⓘ Hong Kong & Kowloon Ferry (☎ 2815 6063)

⑤ Yung Shue Wan/Sok Kwu Wan to: Central ($10-20), Aberdeen ($7-12)

✕ Bookworm Café, Yung Shue Wan Main St (organic); Tai Yuen, 15 First St, Sok Kwu Wan (seafood)

### Lamma to Aberdeen Loop

You can make a nice round trip by catching the ferry to Yung Shue Wan, walking across the island to Sok Kwu Wan and then catching the ferry to Aberdeen. As you enter Aberdeen Harbour, you'll see as much boat life as you would on a sampan ride.

This is a nice place to relax, despite the clear view of the power station. You soon come to a ridge where you can look down on Sok Kwu Wan, a small place supporting a dozen or more fine waterfront seafood restaurants.

## Stanley    (2, E4)

About 2000 people lived at Stanley when the British took over in 1841, making it one of the island's largest settlements at the time. The British built a prison near the village in 1937 – just in time to be used by the Japanese to intern the expatriates. It's still used as a prison.

The main attraction is **Stanley Market** (p. 40) and the local restaurants; there's an OK **beach** where you can rent windsurfers. At the western end of the bay is **Murray House**, moved brick by brick from the current Bank of China site and newly opened as a restaurant complex (p. 80). Visit Stanley during the week: it's bursting with tourists and locals on weekends.

### INFORMATION

*15km south of Central*

🚌 6, 66, 262 (from Exchange Sq)

✕ Lucy's (p. 80); El Cid Caramar (p. 80)

Isn't it ionic: stately Murray House (1846)

# Lantau Island (1, G2)

Lantau is 142 sq km, almost twice the size of Hong Kong Island. More than half of this sparsely populated mountainous island has been declared country parks. There are good hikes, interesting villages and monasteries.

A great 5-6hr trip can be made by taking the ferry to Mui Wo then bus 2 to the Buddhist **Po Lin Monastery**, situated in the village of Ngong Ping. On a hill above the monastery is the **Tiantan Buddha Statue**, a 22m bronze beauty. As well as the worthwhile climb to the base of the Buddha there are superb views over central Lantau and monastery grounds to explore. From here take bus 21 to the fishing town of **Tai O** on Lantau's west coast, where traditional stilt houses can still be seen. Walk over the small iron bridge that connects the island town to the mainland, and at Fook Lam Moon restaurant turn right and walk past stilt houses to **Hau Wong Temple**. From Tai O take bus 1 back to Mui Wo or bus 11 over the steep interior to Tung Chung, where you

*20-30km west of Central*
- Tung Chung; Airport
- Central/Tsim Sha Tsui–Mui Wo
- First Ferry Co (☎ 2131 8181); CPA (parks info; ☎ 2422 9431; e parks.afcd.gov.hk)
- ferry $15-31; buses $9-15; MTR $18
- ✕ Po Lin Vegetarian Restaurant, Po Lin Monastery; Fook Lam Moon, Tai O (seafood); The Stoep, Lwr Cheung Sha Village (Sth African on the beach)

*Inscription: Po Lin Monastery*

can see how a small town changes when an international airport sprouts up next door. There's an MTR station at Tung Chung to take you back to the city.

If you're keen for a dip take bus 4 to **Cheung Sha**, a 3km sandy stretch divided into lower Cheung Sha and the prettier upper Cheung Sha.

The 70km-long **Lantau Trail** loops around the island from Mui Wo. The middle section of the trail (the most scenic part) is accessible from Po Lin at Ngong Ping. It's 17.5km (or 7hrs) from Ngong Ping to Mui Wo, via Lantau and Sunset Peaks. The airport adjoins Lantau so you can work in a trip to the island's attractions with your arrival or departure from Hong Kong.

*Interior: Po Lin (Precious Lotus) Monastery*

## Sai Kung     (1, D8)

The Sai Kung Peninsula is the last chunk of Hong Kong, apart from the outlying islands, that remains a haven for hikers, swimmers and boating enthusiasts. Decades ago, pirates and tigers roamed the peninsula. These days, the occasional stray dogs might be a walker's only worry. Sai Kung town is an excellent point to set off from and then return to for delicious seafood on the waterfront in the evening. This is also the departure point for the Kau Sai Chau Island golf course (p. 44).

**INFORMATION**

*25km northeast of Central*

🚌 Choi Hung MTR then Public Light bus 1 (20mins), or bus 92 (30mins) to Sai Kung town. Change to bus 94 for Sai Kung East Country Park and the Maclehose Trail.

ⓘ CPA (☎ 2422 9431; 🖲 parks.afcd.gov.hk)

🕐 Visitor Centre: Wed-Mon 9.30am-4.30pm

✖ Chuen Kee (p. 79)

A short journey to any of the islands off Sai Kung town is rewarding. Hidden away are some excellent beaches that are worth visiting on a *kaido* (small boat). *Kaidos* leave from the waterfront in Sai Kung town. Most head over to **Sharp Island** (Kiu Tsui Chau) about 1.5km away. Hap Mun Bay, a sandy beach in the south of the island, is served, as is Kiu Tsui Bay to the west.

The **Maclehose Trail**, a 100km route across the New Territories, begins near Sai Kung at Pak Tam Chung (1, D9), where the first few km of the trail reveal fantastic coastal scenery. There's also a wheelchair-accessible picnic area and a visitor centre here.

## Shek O     (2, D5)

Shek O has one of the best beaches on Hong Kong Island. The village is small, so it's easy to get your bearings. Between the bus stop and the beach you'll pass some restaurants; if you take the road leading off to the left you'll enter a maze of small homes, which grow in size and luxury as you head along the peninsula. This is the **Shek O headlands**, home to some of Hong Kong's wealthiest families. At the tip of the peninsula there's a lookout over the South China Sea: next stop, the Philippines.

**INFORMATION**

*10km south of Central*

🚌 Shau Kei Wan MTR then bus 9 to To Te Wan, Big Wave Bay & Shek O

ⓘ CPA (☎ 2422 9431; 🖲 parks.afcd.gov.hk)

You can also approach Shek O by foot, along the spectacular **Dragon's Back Trail**. This final 4km of the 50km Hong Kong Trail (p. 25) starts at To Te Wan and takes about 2.5hrs, finishing at the village of Big Wave Bay, 2km north of Shek O. You can have a cooling dip here then walk or take the bus to Shek O.

## Macau                    (7, E1)

Only a 90min ferry ride to the west of Hong Kong, this charming Latin-Asian fusion makes a magnificent getaway. Returned to Chinese sovereignty in 1999 after some 450 years under Portuguese rule, Macau is now a Special Administrative Region of China. This tiny (23.5 sq km) SAR is divided into the Macau Peninsula, which is attached to China, and the islands Taipa and Coloane, connected by bridges. About 95% of the population is Chinese and most tourists are Chinese gamblers drawn to the casinos, but Macau holds some intriguing churches and civil buildings, narrow streets, traditional shops and Portuguese restaurants, making a day trip here far from a gamble. Macau brims with atmosphere and has a labyrinth of backstreets just waiting to be explored.

### INFORMATION

***65km west of Central***

🚢 Macau ferry terminal; Kowloon China ferry terminal (p. 109)

💲 ferry $90-150
Hong Kong dollars are accepted across Macau (except public telephones); Macau patacas are all but impossible to reconvert

ℹ Macau Government Tourist Office (9 Large do Senado; ☎ 853-315 566; **e** www.macautourism.gov.mo) also has an office at the ferry terminal. It may be convenient to visit Macau but you do still need your passport. Central Macau is great to explore on foot, and taxis are cheap for attractions further afield. A taxi between sights listed here would not cost more than $20.

✕ Alfonso III (11a Rua Central; ☎ 853-586 272). This small Portuguese restaurant has won a well-deserved reputation among the Portuguese community. Book ahead.

## Central Macau

### Cemetery of Michael the Archangel

This cemetery, the largest in the region, is smack

*Belo! Largo do Senado*

bang in the centre of the Macau Peninsula. Most of the tombs are baroque ecclesiastical works of art.
✉ **Estrada do Cemitério** 🕐 **10am-6pm** 💲 **free**

### Largo do Senado

'Senate Square' with its wavy black-and-white cobbles and beautiful colonial buildings, is the heart and soul of Macau. The lovely Santa Casa da Misericordia, on the southern side of the square, was a home for orphans and prostitutes in the 18th century. The square and its buildings are illuminated at night.
✉ **Avenida de Almeida**

Ribeiro (opposite Leal Senado)

### Leal Senado

Macau's most important historical building now houses the Provisional Municipal Assembly, an art gallery and the ornately furnished Senate Library. Above the entrance to the garden is a bas-relief of either the Virgin Mary Misericordia or the 16th-century queen Donã Leonor, depending on who you ask.
✉ **163 Avenida de Almeida Ribeiro**
☎ **853-387 333**
🕐 **9am-9pm; library: 1-7pm** 💲 **free**

**Rua de Felicidade**
'The street of happiness' used to be Macau's red-light district. Now the locals come here for a different kind of indulgence. The Macanese sweets sold here can be smelled before they are seen. Grab a few pastries and munch while marvelling at the traditional Chinese architecture in the surrounding area.
✉ **Rua de Felicidade**

**Ruinas de São Paulo (Ruins of St Paul's Cathedral)**
These marvellous ruins were designed by an Italian Jesuit and built by Japanese Christian exiles in the early 1600s. All that remains today is the facade, the mosaic floor and the stone steps. Nevertheless some consider the ruins to be the greatest monument to Christianity in Asia.
✉ **end of Rua da São Paulo**

## Greater Macau, NAPE

**Kun Iam Statue**
Though it sounds naff in the extreme, this 20m-high bronze monument to the goddess of mercy emerging from a lotus is a sublime harbourside sight. Beneath the statue is the **Kun Iam Ecumenical Centre**, a fine place for contemplation.
✉ **Avenida Doutor Sun Yat Sen** ☎ 853-751 516 ◷ **Sat-Thurs 10.30am-6pm** ⑤ free

**Macau Museum of Art**
This is arguably the best place to see both classic and contemporary art in the region (including Hong Kong). It is located in a superb, five-storey complex designed by Bruno Soares, connected by a walkway to the **Macau Cultural Centre**. Permanent museum exhibits include Historical Paintings with works by George Chinnery, excellent calligraphy displays and a magnificent range of Shiwan ceramics. The local and international contemporary exhibits are also of a very high calibre.
✉ **Avenida Xian Xing Hai, S/N, NAPE** ☎ 853-791 9832 ◷ **Tues-Sun 10am-7pm** ⑤ $5

**Macau Tower**
At 338m this is the 10th-tallest free-standing tower in the world. The views across Macau's islands and city centre are spectacular, and the glass floors on the observation deck cause much horror and hilarity.
✉ **Largo da Torre de Macau** ☎ 853-933 339 ◷ **10am-9pm** ⑤ **$45/23 (indoor), $35/18 (outdoor)**

**Maritime Museum**
Home to a world-class collection related to Macau's seafaring past. There's a flower bo at, a Hakka village display and a dragon boat that's still used in races.
✉ **Largo do Pagode da Barra** ☎ 853-595 481 ◷ **Tues-Sun 10am-5.30pm** ⑤ **$10/5 (half-price Sun)**

*The stunning facade of St Paul's Cathedral has come to symbolise Macau*

Jon Davison

# ORGANISED TOURS

Tourism is one of Hong Kong's main money-earners, so it's no surprise that there is a mind-boggling number of tours available. Some of the best tours are offered by the HKTB (☎ 2508 1234; e www.discover hongkong.com), and tours run by separate companies can also be booked through HKTB offices (pp. 112-13).

## Bus Tours

### Deluxe Hong Kong Island Tour

Gray Line, the stalwart tour company, offers a 5hr tour that takes in Man Mo Temple, Victoria Peak, Aberdeen, Stanley and Repulse Bay.
☎ 2368 7111
e www.grayline.com.hk
⏱ 8am, 1pm
$ $290/190

### The Land Between

This 6hr New Territories tour operated by Gray Line takes you to places that are a hassle to get to yourself. Tai Mo Shan (Hong Kong's highest peak) and a village near the mainland border are included.
☎ 2368 7112
⏱ 8.30am
$ $385/335

## Lantau Tours

This 6hr public ferry then bus tour run by Lantau Tours takes you to Lantau Island's beaches, fishing villages and the giant Buddha at Ngong Ping.
☎ 2984 8255
⏱ Mon-Sat 11.45am & 1.45pm; Sun & public holidays noon & 2pm
$ $130

## Boat Tours

### Dolphinwatch

As well as a scenic dolphin-spotting expedition, Dolphinwatch's 4hr tour includes information on the dolphin's plight and Hong Kong's environmental situation. Up to 160 pink dolphins live in Hong Kong's dirty, bustling waters.
☎ 2984 1414

*Taking in the sights, Soho*

e www.hkdolphin watch.com ⏱ Wed, Fri, Sat 8.30am-1pm
$ $320/160

### Harbour & Aberdeen Night Cruise

This 4.5hr, Watertour-run cruise to Aberdeen on a junk includes unlimited drinks and a seafood dinner on a floating restaurant. After dinner you're taken by coach to Stubbs Road Lookout for a view of Hong Kong by night.
☎ 2926 3868
⏱ nightly (hotel pick-up from 5.25pm)
$ $610/510

### Harbour Lights & Lei Yue Mun Seafood Village Dinner Cruise

Catchy name! Watertours offers this 3hr tour including a trip around central Hong Kong Harbour on a

*A feast for the eyes: Aberdeen's floating restaurants*

Chinese junk then a trip to Lei Yue Mun Seafood Village in the Eastern Harbour for a village stroll and seafood banquet.
☎ 2926 3868
e www.watertours hk.com ⊙ 6.15pm
⑤ $390/360

**Harbour Night Cruises**
Two-hour tours run by Splendid Tours skim the neon-saturated shoreline via Kowloon, Causeway Bay and nearby islands. All beer and soft drinks are free onboard.
☎ 2316 2151
e www.splendid tours.com ⊙ 9.30pm
⑤ $280/190 (pm)

**Hong Kong Back Garden Tour – Sai Kung**
Jubilee International's 5hr tour of the harbour around Sai Kung takes you by boat to a fish farm, temples and past splendid scenery.
☎ 2530 0500
e www.jubilee.com.hk
⊙ 9am ⑤ $350

## Cultural Kaleidoscope
Another highlight of its excellent services, the HKTB offers a series of free cultural programs in English, 'Meet the People', run by the city's cultural connoisseurs and experts.

- Taijiquan — introductory class
- Guided Architecture Tour — guided tour
- Heritage & Architecture Walks — walking tour
- Chinese Antiques — appreciation class
- Chinese Tea — appreciation class
- Pearl Grading — appreciation class
- Jade Grading — appreciation class
- Chinese Clothing — appreciation class
- Fung Shui — introductory class
- 'The Hong Kong Story' Exhibition — guided tour
- Duk Ling Ride (Chinese Junk) — tour
- Cantonese Opera — appreciation class
- Kung Fu Corner — introductory class

## Sport Tours
**Come Horseracing**
Splendid Tours offers 5.5hr (night) and 7hr (day) trips to race meetings at Happy Valley, Hong Kong Island and Sha Tin. Tours include coach transfers from hotels, entry to the Hong Kong Jockey Club Members' Enclosure and meals. If you gamble, the Jockey Club takings go to charity.
☎ 2316 2151
e www.splendid-tours.com ⊙ Wed evenings & Sat ⑤ $490 (must be over 18yo)

*A fun, family day out at lovely Lantau Island*

# shopping

Shopping in Hong Kong goes way beyond buying stuff you need: it's a social activity, a favourite recreation, an after-hours release. And though it isn't the bargain basement it once was, Honkers still wins for variety and its passionate embrace of competitive consumerism. Any international brand worthy of its own perfume sets up shop here, and there are a slew of local brands worth your money too. Clothing, jewellery and electronics are the city's strong suits – all of them can be made to order, whether it's an Armani-copy ensemble, a pair of earrings or a PC.

## Smart Buying

Most shops are loath to give refunds but they can usually be persuaded to exchange untampered purchases: make sure you get a detailed receipt that enumerates the goods as well as the payment. When buying electronics, always beware of goods imported by a nonauthorised agent, as this may void your warranty. If you have trouble with dodgy merchants in Hong Kong, call the Consumer Council on ☎ 2929 2222.

*Nathan Rd shops (caveat emptor)*

## Shopping Areas

The main shopping areas are Tsim Sha Tsui, Central and Causeway Bay. **Nathan Rd**, Tsim Sha Tsui, is the main tourist strip, and the only place where you'll find spruikers. It's also the place you're most likely to get ripped off, especially on electronics or cameras. **Central** has a mix of mid-range to top-end shopping centres and street-front retail; it's popular with locals and tourists. This is a good area to look for cameras, books, antiques and designer threads. **Causeway Bay** is a crush of department stores and smaller outlets selling eclectic fashion. For market shopping see page 40.

## Opening Hours

You can more or less expect shops to be open from 10am to 6pm daily. In Causeway Bay and Wan Chai, many will stay open until 9.30pm. In Tsim Sha Tsui and Yau Ma Tei, shops close around 9pm. If shops take a day off, it's usually Monday; they may also be closed Sunday morning.

## Paying & Bargaining

There are no sales taxes so the marked price is the price you'll pay. Credit cards are widely accepted, except in markets. It's rare for traders to accept travellers cheques or foreign currency as payment. Sales assistants in department or chain stores rarely have any leeway to give discounts but you can try bargaining in owner-operated shops and certainly in markets. If you've loaded up big, shops will usually be happy to ship items home for you.

# DEPARTMENT STORES

## Lane Crawford (6, B5)

The original branch of Hong Kong's first Western-style department store. It's still an upscale place but doesn't have the prestige of the early days. There are other branches in Pacific Place, Admiralty (4, G9); and Times Square, Causeway Bay (5, G2).

✉ **70 Queen's Rd, Central** ☎ **2118 3388**
Ⓜ **Central** Ⓠ **yes**
🕐 **10am-7.30pm**

## Marks & Spencer

**(3, H3)** Britain's well-known chain is a good place for undies, simple coordinates, sensible shoes and accessories like sun-hats and brollies. There's a scattering of branches including Pacific Place, Admiralty (4, G9); Pearl City Plaza, Causeway Bay (5, E3); Times Square, Causeway Bay (5, G2); and Central Tower, Central (4, E5).

✉ **Ocean Centre, Canton Rd, Tsim Sha Tsui**

## Fashionistas & Outlet Hounds

Hong Kong pretties up for Fashion Week in mid-July. The main parades and events are at the Convention & Exhibition Centre (4, D12) but look out for well-dressed shindigs in shopping centres around town. Mid-July is also sale season, lasting until the end of August (sales also occur just after Chinese New Year).

If you are shopping at the other end of the scale, snap up the book *The Smart Shopper in Hong Kong* by Carolyn Radin to help you bargain hunt.

☎ **2926 3346**
Ⓜ **Tsim Sha Tsui**
🕐 **10am-7pm**

## Sogo (5, F3)

This Japanese-owned store is the hub of Causeway Bay, with 12 well-organised floors. The range is mind-boggling: over 20 brands of neckties just for starters. Eclectic departments include the 'baby train models' area and a culture centre with patchwork and oil paintings.

✉ **555 Hennessy Rd,**
**Causeway Bay** ☎ **2833 8338** Ⓜ **Causeway Bay**
Ⓠ **yes** 🕐 **11am-11pm**

## Wing On (4, C3)

This Hong Kong department store is notable for being locally owned but in the end it's nothing particularly extraordinary. There's another branch at 345 Nathan Rd, Jordan (3, B4).

✉ **211 Des Voeux Rd, Central** ☎ **2852 1888**
Ⓜ **Central** Ⓠ **yes**
🕐 **10am-7.30pm**

## Mall Trawl

Hong Kong is mall-rat heaven but don't feel compelled to visit more than a couple: the same brands turn up over and over again. They include:

**Festival Walk** (2, A3) 80 Tat Chee Ave, Kowloon Tong – a new centre with a good middle-rung selection of shops, great disabled access and toilets on every level.

**Harbour City** (3, H3) Canton Rd, Tsim Sha Tsui – the biggest by far with 700 shops in four zones.

**International Finance Centre (IFC) Mall** (4, D6) 1 Harbour View St, Central – a bright new centre with high-fashion boutiques, the great Eating Plus snackery and the airport railway terminal downstairs.

**The Landmark** (4, E5) 1 Pedder St, Central – high fashion and good food in a pleasant open space. Many high-end international brands are represented.

**Pacific Place** (4, G9) 88 Queensway, Admiralty – see page 61.

**Prince's Building** (4, E6) 10 Chater Rd, Central – poky and disorienting but worth a look for its speciality fashion, toy and kitchenware shops.

**Times Square** (5, G2) 1 Matheson St, Causeway Bay – a dozen floors of retail organised by type. There's electronics (on 7th), a play area (on 9th) and food (on 12th & 13th).

# CLOTHING

**Blanc De Chine** (4, E5)
♀♂ A sumptuous shop that specialises in traditional Chinese jackets, off the rack or made to measure. There's also a lovely selection of silk dresses.
✉ Shop 201, Pedder Bldg, 12 Pedder St, Central ☎ 2524 7875
🚇 Central 🚻 yes
🕙 Mon-Sat noon-7pm, Sun noon-5pm

**Dada Cabaret Voltaire** (5, F3) ♀
Ragged rainbow colours that are also sported by the staff. Just one of many fine shops in the Fashion Island complex.
✉ Shop F-13a, Fashion Island, 19 Great George St, Causeway Bay
☎ 2890 1708
🚇 Causeway Bay
🚻 yes 🕙 noon-10pm

**Dong Ng** (3, F7) ♂
Small shop with large range of stylish suits. It's an all-in-one tailor-seller affair.
✉ Shop 39, Beverley Commercial Centre, 87-105 Chatham Rd, Tsim Sha Tsui 🚇 Tsim Sha Tsui 🚌 5, 5C, 8, 8A
🕙 4-10pm

**Encyco** (5, E3) ♀
Independent young Hong Kong designer with an eye for wispy wear, verging on the wacky.
✉ Shop 182, Island Beverley, 1 Great George St, Causeway Bay 🚇 Causeway Bay
🚻 yes 🕙 1.30-10.30pm

**Garex Ison** (6, D5) ♀
A local designer working with textures and layers to come up with stylish suits,

*China chic – Central*

tops and bottoms. One of a few frolicsome mid-market fashion outlets in this strip.
✉ 44 Lan Kwai Fong, Central ☎ 2537 3326
🚇 Central 🚻 yes
🚌 13, 26, 43 🕙 Mon-Sat 11am-8pm

**Helmut Lang** (4, E5) ♀♂
Like shopping in the brain of a German avant-garde artist. Behind the black slab facade are both formal and casual clothes and accessories.
✉ Shop 228, The Landmark, Central
☎ 2869 5571
🚇 Central 🚻 yes
🕙 Mon-Sat 10am-7.30pm, Sun 11am-7pm

**i.t** (3, F5) ♀♂
This shop and the b+ab shop next door both sell the cute, trendy gear that abounds in Hong Kong. There are i.t and I.T shops in the major shopping areas (capitalisation denotes its 'grown-up' range).
✉ Shop 1030, Miramar Centre, 1-23 Kimberley Rd, Tsim Sha Tsui
☎ 2736 9152 🚇 Tsim Sha Tsui 🕙 noon-10pm

## Alt Malls

Crammed in buildings, up escalators and in back lanes are Hong Kong's malls of micro-shops selling designer threads, a kaleidoscope of kooky accessories and an Imelda of funky footwear. The best shopping is done from 3pm to 10pm, when all shops are open.

**Beverley Commercial Centre** (3, F7)
✉ 87-105 Chatham Rd, Tsim Sha Tsui
🚇 Tsim Sha Tsui 🚌 5, 5C, 8, 8A

**Island Beverley** (5, E3)
✉ 1 Great George St, Causeway Bay
🚇 Causeway Bay 🚻 yes

**Rise Building** (3, F6)
✉ 5-11 Granville Circuit, Tsim Sha Tsui
🚇 Tsim Sha Tsui 🚌 5, 5C, 8, 8A

**Trendy Zone**
✉ Chow Tai Fook Centre, 580a Nathan Rd, Mong Kok (p. 47) 🚇 Mong Kok, Yau Ma Tei 🚌 1, 1A, 2, 6, 6C

**Update Mall** (3, H5)
✉ 36-44 Nathan Rd, Tsim Sha Tsui 🚇 Tsim Sha Tsui

**Joyce Ma** (4, F5) ♀
Issey Miyake, Yves Saint Laurent, Jean Paul Gaultier, Commes des Garçons, Voyage and Yohji Yamamoto are just some whose wearable wares are on display here. Also at Pacific Place, Admiralty (4, G9); and 23 Nathan Rd, Tsim Sha Tsui (3, H5).
✉ **New World Tower, 16 Queen's Rd Central, Central** ☎ **2810 1120**
🚇 Central 🚃 yes
🕐 Mon-Sat 10.30am-7.30pm, Sun noon-6pm

**Kent & Curwen** (4, G9) ♂
Distinguished suits, dress shirts, cufflinks and casual tops for the gentleman who'd rather look to the manor born than dotcom upstart.
✉ **Shop 372, Pacific Place, 88 Queensway, Admiralty** ☎ **2840 0023** 🚇 Admiralty
🚃 yes 🕐 10am-7.30pm

**Labels for Less** (4, D6) ♀♂ If you've already bought up at **Swank** (shops at Landmark, Pacific Place, New World Centre) it could be upsetting to come here. Often the difference with the so-called seconds sold at this shop is the price. There's another outlet at the Ocean Terminal, Tsim Sha Tsui (3, J2).
✉ **Shop 3008, IFC Mall, 1 Harbour View St, Central** ☎ **2295 3883** 🚇 Central
🕐 11am-8pm

**Miu Miu** (4, E5) ♀
Super-cute and creative threads for neo-adults ('oh they put a zip *there*'). The shoes here are

exceptionally stylish.
✉ **Shop B24, The Landmark, 1 Pedder St, Central** ☎ **2523 7833**
🚇 Central 🚃 yes
🕐 Mon-Sat 10am-7pm, Sun 11am-6pm

**Onitsuka** (3, E6) ♀♂
Basic black threaded with trinkets, eyelets, studs and general naughtiness. Be made up, waxed, shaved and ready to party.
✉ **15c Austin Ave, Tsim Sha Tsui** ☎ **2368 1085** 🚇 Tsim Sha Tsui
🕐 Mon-Sat noon-8pm

**Pro Cam-Fis** (3, J2) ♀♂
Outdoor gear, both light-weight and cold weather, including kids' sizes. There's a good range of Eagle Creek travel products.
✉ **Shop 148, Ocean Terminal, Canton Rd, Tsim Sha Tsui** ☎ **2736 1382** 🚇 Tsim Sha Tsui
🕐 10am-7pm

**Shanghai Tang** (4, E5) ♀♂ Started by flamboyant Hong Kong businessman David Tang, Shanghai Tang sparked something of a fashion wave in Hong Kong with its updated versions of traditional Chinese garments. Custom tailoring is available and it has expanded into accessories and gifts.
✉ **Pedder Bldg, 12 Pedder St, Central** ☎ **2525 7333**
🚇 Central 🚃 yes
🕐 Mon-Sat 10am-8pm, Sun noon-6pm (after-noon tea 3-6pm)

**Spy** (5, G2) ♀♂
Tame yet trendy everyday wear such as slacks and short-sleeve shirts. It also has outlets in Rise Building,

Tsim Sha Tsui (3, F6); and the Island Beverley Building, Causeway Bay (5, E3).
✉ **Shop C, 11 Sharp St E, Causeway Bay** ☎ **2893 7799**
🚇 Causeway Bay
🚃 yes 🕐 1-11pm

### Suit Yourself

Need a tailor? Take a walk on Nathan Rd and *they'll* find *you*, or ask your hotel concierge for advice. Otherwise, try **Pacific Custom Tailors** (4, G9; ☎ 2845 5377), Shop 322, Pacific Place, Admiralty, or the unfortunately named **Stitch-Up Tailors** (3, J3; ☎ 2314 4000), Shop 3, Star House, Tsim Sha Tsui. The turnaround on most items is 48hrs, including two fittings.

**Supernova** (3, G6) ♀♂
Smart street wear for the urbane skate freak: shirts, oversized jeans and shoes that look more cool than comfortable. There's also a branch in the Rise Building, Tsim Sha Tsui (3, F6).
✉ **Shop G19, 45-51 Chatham Rd, Tsim Sha Tsui** ☎ **2311 3183**
🚇 Tsim Sha Tsui 🚃 5, 5C, 8, 8A 🕐 2-10pm

**Wanko** (4, E5) ♀
Soft spring colour skirts and blouses as well as sharper business attire. But what we really like about this place is its name. Tell your friends you 'bought it at Wanko'.
✉ **Ground fl, Chinese Bank Bldg, 31-37 Des Vouex Rd** ☎ **2523 0520** 🚇 Central 🚃 yes
🕐 11am-9.30pm

# FOR CHILDREN

**Goody Toys** (4, D6)
Small but select range of high-quality playthings including plenty of educational toys and some that are a plain old lark.
✉ **Shop 2033, IFC Mall, 1 Harbour View St, Central** ☎ 2295 0552 🚇 Central
🕐 10am-8pm

**Kobie Kid'n'Garden** (3, F7) Small shop for smaller people selling cute knits and squeaky footwear.
✉ **Shop 57, Ground fl, Beverley Commercial Centre, 87-105 Chatham Rd, Tsim Sha Tsui** ☎ 2736 1633 🚇 Tsim Sha Tsui 🚌 5, 5C, 8, 8A 🕐 3-10pm

**Mothercare** (4, E6)
Baby gear, supplies for mums and dads (prams, bouncers, bottles), plus toys for tots. Most of the stock is imported from Europe.
✉ **Shop 338, Prince's Bldg, 10 Chater Rd, Central** ☎ 2523 5704 🚇 Central 🚌 yes 🕐 10am-6pm

**Ocean Boutique** (3, H6) Kiddies gear made in China and Korea, much of it with funny English misspellings. The jumpsuits promise rumpus, while the formal dresses are both tragic and gigglesome.
✉ **1 Minden Ave, Tsim Sha Tsui** ☎ 2366 0889 🚇 Tsim Sha Tsui 🚌 5, 5C, 8, 8A 🕐 Mon-Sat 10am-7pm

**Toto** (4, E6)
Jumpsuits and other togs for under-2s; everything made by this Hong Kong brand is 100% cotton.
✉ **Shop 212, Prince's Bldg, 10 Chater Rd, Central** ☎ 2869 4668 🚇 Central 🚌 yes 🕐 10am-7pm

**Toy Museum** (4, E6)
Top-of-the-line teddy bears, action men, beanie babies and Pokemon paraphernalia. There's a great collection of old GI Joes for dads to amuse themselves with.
✉ **Shop 320, Prince's Bldg, 10 Chater Rd, Central** ☎ 2869 9138 🚇 Central 🚌 yes

## Smells Like Teen Shoppers

Younger shoppers may enjoy the colour and choice of shopping areas listed in Alt Malls (p. 58), especially Update Mall. This is where Hong Kong's youngest mall-trawlers go for clothes, trinkets and to capture the moment on sticker machines.

🕐 Mon-Sat 10am-7pm, Sun noon-7pm

**Wise Kids** (4, G9)
Nothing to plug in, nothing with batteries: Wise Kids concentrates on kids generating energy with their necktop unit. As well as stuffed toys, card games and things to build, there are practical items for parents, like toilet-lid locks and carry-alls.
✉ **Shop 134, Pacific Place, 88 Queensway, Admiralty** ☎ 2868 0133 🚇 Admiralty 🚌 yes 🕐 10.30am-7.30pm

*With a pout like that, you're going a long way, kid*

# JEWELLERY & COSMETICS

### Amours Antiques
(6, C2) Twentieth-century wearable antiques like rhinestone jewellery, frocks and a darling clutch of beaded and tapestry bags. Most wares date from 1910-40. A second branch holds forth in the Galleria, Central (4, F6).
✉ 45 Staunton St, Soho ☎ 2803 7877 ⓰ Central, Sheung Wan ⏰ Mon-Sat 2-8pm

### Georg Jensen (3, J5)
Jensen's specialises in expertly crafted silver. The jewellery is exquisite, but it's in the liquid-looking ornaments and perfectly weighted cutlery that the Danish designer's imagination really seems to spark.
✉ Shop BL2, The Peninsula, cnr Salisbury & Nathan Rds, Tsim Sha Tsui ☎ 2724 1510 ⓰ Tsim Sha Tsui ⏰ Mon-Sat 10am-6.30pm

### J's (3, J2)
Affordable jewellery for those who like to gleam without being ostentatious. Most pieces are silver but some feature small diamonds; there's a groovy range of sunglasses. There are a dozen shops around town.
✉ Shop 2217, Ocean Terminal, Canton Rd, Tsim Sha Tsui ☎ 2736 8464 ⓰ Tsim Sha Tsui ⏰ 10am-7pm

### King Fook (4, D5)
The most fantastic-looking shop in the reputable King Fook jewellery chain is worth visiting for its sheer garishness. There are branches in Pacific Place, Admiralty (4, G9); HK Mansion, 1 Yee Wo St, Causeway Bay (5, F3); and Miramar Hotel, Tsim Sha Tsui (3, F5).
✉ 30-32 Des Voeux Rd, Central ☎ 2822 8573 ⓰ Central ⏰ yes ⏰ 9.30am-7pm

### King Sing Jewellers
(3, J3) A long-standing jewellers with a wide selection of diamonds, pearls and gold items. The sales staff are pleasantly un-pushy.
✉ Shop 14, Star House, 3 Salisbury Rd, Tsim Sha Tsui ☎ 2735 7021 ⓰ Tsim Sha Tsui ⏰ 10am-7.30pm

### My Moody Lazy Cat
(3, F7) Good range of locally made jewellery, some of which looks like it came from a monopoly board.
✉ Shop 59, Beverley Commercial Centre, 87-105 Chatham Rd, Tsim Sha Tsui ☎ 2302 1236 ⓰ Tsim Sha Tsui ⏰ 5, 5C, 8, 8A ⏰ 3-10pm

### Premier Jewellery
(3, H5) Third-generation family firm directed by a qualified gemmologist. The selection isn't huge but if you're looking for something particular, give them a day's notice to have a selection ready for your arrival. Henry Cheng and team will also help you create your own designs.
✉ Shop G16, Holiday Inn Golden Mile, 50 Nathan Rd, Tsim Sha Tsui ☎ 2368 0003 ⓰ Tsim Sha Tsui

⏰ Mon-Sat 10am-7.30pm, Sun 10.30am-4pm

### Shu Uemura Beauty Boutique (4, G9)
The place to come for mauve eyelashes, spangly nail polish and rust lipstick as well as a deluxe range of make-up brushes, soothing bath tonics and skincare advice. There are branches in The Landmark, Central (4, E5); and Times Square (5, G2).
✉ Shop 129, Pacific Place, 88 Queensway, Admiralty ☎ 2918 1238 ⓰ Admiralty ⏰ yes ⏰ 10.30am-8pm

### Shopping Sight
**Pacific Place (4, G9)**
Hong Kong's premiere shopping complex is an impressive feat of organised form. Although typical of the city's large-scale commercial developments, the complex's originality of shape and style reveal novel solutions to the island's perennial space problem. The harmonious outlines of Phase II buildings (the Island Shangri-La and Conrad hotels) soften the hard angles of Phase I (shops and cinemas) and add beauty, balance and a skerrick of mystery into the crush of surrounding skyscrapers.
✉ 88 Queensway, Admiralty ⓰ Admiralty ⏰ yes

# BOOKS

### Bookazine (4, E6)
Operates atmosphere-free chain stores dotted all around Hong Kong. Each shop stocks a dependable range of books, magazines and stationery.
✉ **Shop 327-329, Prince's Bldg, 10 Chater Rd, Central** ☎ 2522 1785 ⊕ **Central** 🚻 **yes** ⏰ Mon-Sat 9am-7pm, Sun 10am-6pm

### Cosmos Books
(4, G11) This shop has a good selection of Chinese-related books in the basement. Upstairs there are English-language books (nonfiction is quite strong) plus one of the city's best stationery departments.
✉ **15 Johnston Rd, Wan Chai** ☎ 2866 1677 ⊕ **Wan Chai** 🚻 **yes** 🚌 **37B, 75, 90** ⏰ 10am-8pm

### Dymocks (4, D6)
Australia's Dymocks chain offers a solid mainstream selection of page-turners,

travel books and mags. There's a smaller branch in Central's Star Ferry concourse (4, D7).
✉ **Shop 2007-2011, IFC Mall, 1 Harbour View St, Central** ☎ 2117 0360 ⊕ **Central** ⏰ Mon-Sat 9am-9pm, Sun 10am-8.30pm

### Film Buff (3, A3)
Weeny shop in the Broadway cinema complex with a great range of kooky local zines and odd-ball film paraphernalia. Also check out the **Kubrick** shop next door for glossy art books, CDs and expensive coffee.
✉ **3 Public Sq St, Broadway Cinemateque, Yau Ma Tei** ☎ 2782 5879 ⊕ **Yau Ma Tei** ⏰ 2-10pm

### Flow (6, C3)
Exchange/second-hand bookshop with a focus on spiritual literature. Meditation workshops are occasionally run; for these

*Kubrick bookshop*

you'll need to levitate to the 2nd floor.
✉ **L1, Lyndhurst Tce, Central (enter from Cochrane St)** ☎ 2964 9483 ⊕ **Central, Sheung Wan** ⏰ noon-7pm

### Hong Kong Book Centre (4, D5)
This basement shop has a vast selection of books and magazines, including a mammoth number of business titles. There's another pleasantly cluttered branch in the basement of The Landmark, Central (4, E5).
✉ **On Lok Yuen Bldg, 25 Des Voeux Rd Central, Central** ☎ 2522 7064 ⊕ **Central** ⏰ Mon-Fri 9am-6.30pm, Sat 9am-5.30pm, Sun (summer only) 1-5pm

### Joint Publishing Company (6, A5)
Joint Publishing (opposite the Central Market) is out-standing for books about China and books and tapes for studying Chinese lan-guages. Most English titles, including the patchy but creditable literature section,

## Recommended Reading
One of the best history books is Jan Morris' *Hong Kong – Epilogue to an Empire. The Last Governor* is Jonathan Dimbleby's acclaimed account of Chris Patten's historic mission to Hong Kong. *Culture Shock! Hong Kong – A Guide to Customs and Etiquette* by Betty Wei & Elizabeth Li is an excellent introduction to Hong Kong culture. Edward Stokes' *Exploring Hong Kong's Countryside* is a good resource for hikers and nature-lovers. The most famous novel set in Hong Kong is *The World of Suzie Wong*, written in 1957 by Richard Mason and set in seedy Wan Chai. *Planet Hong Kong: Popular Cinema and the Art of Entertainment* is David Bordwell's somewhat academic investigation of the art and cul-ture of Hong Kong movies.

are on the mezzanine.
✉ **9 Queen Victoria St, Central** ☎ **2868 6844** Ⓜ Central, Sheung Wan ⏱ Mon-Fri 10.30am-7.30pm, Sat 11am-9pm, Sun 1-6pm

**Kelly & Walsh (4, G9)**
A smart shop with a good selection of art, design and culinary books. The children's books are shelved in a handy kids' reading lounge.
✉ **Shop 304, Pacific Place, 88 Queensway, Admiralty** ☎ **2522 5743** Ⓜ Admiralty ⏱ Mon-Sat 9.30am-8pm, Sun 11am-8pm

**Page One (3, H3)**
A chain, yes, but one with attitude. Page One has Hong Kong's best selection of art and design magazines and books; it's also strong on photography, literature, film and children's books. There's another big branch in Festival Walk, Kowloon Tong.
✉ **Shop 3002, Harbour City, Canton Rd, Tsim Sha Tsui** ☎ **2730 6080** Ⓜ Tsim Sha Tsui ⏱ noon-10pm

**Professional Bookshop (4, E6)**
This shop carries an excellent selection of business, legal and professional titles. It's a good place to get grounded in business-speak, Hong Kong style.
✉ **Shop 104a,** **Alexandra House, 16-20 Chater Rd, Central** ☎ **2526 5387** Ⓜ Central 🚇 yes ⏱ Mon-Fri 9am-6.30pm, Sat 9am-5.30pm

**Swindon Books (3, H4)** Swindon, behind the Hyatt Regency, is one of Hong Kong's larger booksellers. There are branches in the Ocean Terminal, Tsim Sha Tsui (3, J2); the Ocean Centre, Tsim Sha Tsui (3, H3); and the Star Ferry terminal, Tsim Sha Tsui (3, K3).
✉ **13-15 Lock Rd, Tsim Sha Tsui** ☎ **2366 8001** Ⓜ Tsim Sha Tsui ⏱ Mon-Sat 9am-6.30pm, Sun 12.30-6.30pm

# MUSIC

**CD Exchange of Hong Kong (2, B2)**
Elevator-sized shop crammed in a basement full of CD outlets with a wide selection of styles. CD Exchange stocks alternative pop and sells both second-hand and new discs.
✉ **Shop B8, Sino Centre, 582-592 Nathan Rd, Mong Kok (p. 47)** ☎ **2782 1692** Ⓜ Mong Kok, Yau Ma Tei 🚌 1, 1A, 2, 6, 6A, 6C ⏱ 1-9pm

**HMV (4, E5)**
If you're not after anything too obscure, HMV will probably satisfy with its good range of CDs, DVDs and magazines. There are branches in Windsor House, Causeway Bay (5, F4); and the Sands Building, Tsim Sha Tsui (3, H4).
✉ **Central Bldg,** **1-3 Pedder St, Central** ☎ **2739 0268** Ⓜ Central ⏱ 9am-10pm

**Hong Kong Records (4, G9)** Local outfit with a good selection of Cantonese and international sounds, including Chinese traditional, jazz, classical and contemporary music. There's also a good range of VCDs of both Chinese and Western movies (with Chinese subtitles).
✉ **Shop 252, Pacific Place, 88 Queensway, Admiralty** ☎ **2845 7088** Ⓜ Admiralty 🚇 yes ⏱ Sun-Wed 10am-8pm, Thurs-Sat 10am-9pm

**Monitor Records (3, D5)** One of Hong Kong's only dedicated independent music shops is a well-presented operation that specialises in indie and imported sounds that you wouldn't even bother asking for elsewhere. Check the local alternative section for a true aural souvenir.
✉ **Shop 5, Fortune Terrace, 4-16 Tak Shing St, Kowloon** ☎ **2809 4603** Ⓜ Jordan ⏱ noon-10pm

CD standby HMV

# FOOD & TOBACCO

### Aji Ichiban (5, G2)
One of a chain of shops selling exotic dried fruit (sour plum, 10-scent olive) and the freaky dried seafood you see at the markets, but here with English labels (shredded squid, eel slices) and nibble-sized tasting portions.
✉ **Shop 1037, Times Square, 1 Matheson St, Causeway Bay** ☎ **2506 1516** Ⓜ **Causeway Bay** 🚌 **yes** 🕐 **10am-7pm**

### CitySuper (5, G2)
Gourmet supermarket with ready-to-eats like sushi and salads and lots of fresh pro-duce flown in at exorbitant prices. Even if you're not shopping, you can browse and be glad you're not pay-ing $60 for a bunch of leeks back home. Also at Harbour City, Tsim Sha Tsui (3, H3).
✉ **Times Square, 1 Matheson St, Causeway Bay** ☎ **2506 2888** Ⓜ **Causeway Bay** 🚌 **yes** 🕐 **Sun-Thurs 10.30am-10pm, Fri-Sat 10.30am-11pm**

### Fook Ming Tong Tea Shop (4, E5)
Carefully chosen teas and tea-making accoutrements. There's even a 'solitary tea', which tastes appropriately bitter. There are other shops,

*Dried fish, Sheung Wan*

*Try before you buy at the Lock Cha Tea Shop*

including one in Sogo, Causeway Bay (5, F3); and another in Ocean Terminal, Tsim Sha Tsui (5, F3).
✉ **Shop G3-4, The Landmark, 1 Pedder St, Central** ☎ **2521 0337** Ⓜ **Central** 🕐 **Mon-Sat 10am-7.30pm, Sun 11am-6pm**

### Lock Cha Tea Shop (4, D2)
Our favourite shop (enter from Ladder St) for Chinese teas, tea sets, wooden tea-boxes and well-presented gift packs of vari-ous cuppas. You can try before you buy.
✉ **290b Queen's Rd Central, Sheung Wan** ☎ **2805 1360** Ⓜ **Sheung Wan** 🚌 **26** 🕐 **11am-7pm**

### Minamoto Kitchoan (6, C4)
These folk go to unbelievable bother to make sweets so intricate that eating them seems crude. Do it anyway and try the *tousenka* (a big peach whose stone is replaced by a baby green peach).
✉ **Shop B, Winway Bldg, 50 Wellington St, Central** ☎ **2577 5702** Ⓜ **Central** 🚌 **yes**

🕐 **Mon-Sat 10am-9pm, Sun 10am-8pm**

### Oliver's (4, E6)
The wood-panelled floors set the tone: this ain't no ordinary supermarket. Matzos or Mexican hot sauce? Got it. There's also a great range of international beers and the imported fruit and vegies obviously come first class.
✉ **Shop 201, Prince's Bldg, 10 Chater Rd, Central** ☎ **2869 5119** Ⓜ **Central** 🚌 **yes** 🕐 **9am-8pm**

### Tabaqueria Filipina (4, E6)
Sometimes you do need a fat cigar to feel like you're making it in the big city. This boxy shop comes to the rescue with Cuban, Dominican and other fine chompers. There are other branches at 30 Wyndham St, Central (4, E5); and Convention Plaza, Wan Chai (4, E12).
✉ **Shop 105, Alexandra House, 6 Ice House St, Central** ☎ **2877 1541** Ⓜ **Central** 🚌 **yes** 🕐 **Mon-Fri 10am-7.30pm, Sat 10am-6.30pm**

# COMPUTERS & ELECTRONICS

**1010** (3, G3)
The latest, smallest, sleekest in mobile phones and palm pilots – pure binary finery. There's another branch at Century Square, Central (6, C5).
✉ **82-84 Canton Rd, Tsim Sha Tsui** ☎ **2910 1010** Ⓜ **Tsim Sha Tsui** ⊘ **10am-7pm**

**Chung Yuen Electrical Co** (4, E6)
Fair-minded, fixed-price electronics shop with a good selection of DVD players, sound systems, monitors and organisers. The shop is small but the gear is good.
✉ **Shop 227, Prince's Bldg, 10 Chater Rd, Central** ☎ **2524 8066** Ⓜ **Central** 🚊 **yes** ⊘ **10am-7pm**

**Houston Crest** (3, J3)
Slick collection of desktops, laptops and PDAs, but for many travellers it will be the accessories that prove handy. Modem protectors, various adaptors and cables could be what you need to get roadworthy. There are other outlets in Harbour City, Tsim Sha Tsui (3, H3); and Windsor House, Causeway Bay (5, F4).
✉ **Shop D1, Star House, 3 Salisbury Rd, Tsim Sha Tsui** ☎ **2730 4382** Ⓜ **Tsim Sha Tsui** ⊘ **10am-6pm**

**Winframe System** (2, B2) This is just one of your options in the overwhelming Mong Kok Computer Centre – three floors packed with shops selling software and hardware: modems, processors, digital cameras, disk drives, laptops and

**Circuitry Circus**
The **Golden Building Shopping Centre** (2, A2; opposite Sham Shui Po MTR exit D), 146-152 Fuk Wah St, Sham Shui Po, is the place for cheap software of somewhat dubious origin, games and accessories like keyboards, printer cartridges and disks. Most shops open daily 10am-9pm but some don't open until noon. It's packed on weekends.

computer manuals.
✉ **Shop 106, Mong Kok Computer Centre, 8 Nelson St, Mong Kok (p. 47)** ☎ **2300 1238** Ⓜ **Mong Kok** ⊘ **1-10pm**

# PHOTOGRAPHIC EQUIPMENT

**Color Six** (6, C5)
Reliable photo processing (slides take just 3hrs) and professional film for sale. Prices aren't the lowest in town but the service is top quality.
✉ **Shell Bldg, 18a Stanley St, Lan Kwai Fong** ☎ **2542 2677** Ⓜ **Central** ⊘ **Mon-Fri 8am-7pm, Sat 8am-5pm**

**Hing Lee Camera Company** (6, B3)
Hing Lee is a reputable photographic supply outlet. Come here for new and second-hand 35mm camera bodies and lenses and mid-range compact cameras.
✉ **25 Lyndhurst Tce, Lan Kwai Fong** ☎ **2544 7593** Ⓜ **Central** ⊘ **Mon-Sat 9.30am-7pm**

**Photo Scientific** (6, C5)
The favourite of Hong Kong's professionals. You may find cheaper equipment elsewhere, but Photo Scientific has a rock-solid reputation, with labelled prices and no bargaining.
✉ **Eurasia Bldg, 6 Stanley St, Lan Kwai Fong** ☎ **2522 1903** Ⓜ **Central** ⊘ **Mon-Sat 10am-7pm**

## Electric Advice
There are many computer and camera bargains to be had on Nathan Rd, but be warned: many tourists have been had in their hunt for a bargain. Check prices at larger electrical shops like Fortress and Broadway to make sure you're getting a good deal, and check what's in the box before you leave the shop.

# SPORTING EQUIPMENT

### Ahluwalia & Sons

**(3, H4)** This is a shabby but long-established and well-stocked shop flogging golf gear, tennis racquets, cricket bats, shirts and balls. It's cash only and no prices are marked – what further incitement to haggle do you need?

✉ **8c Hankow Rd, Tsim Sha Tsui** ☎ **2368 8334**
🚇 **Tsim Sha Tsui**
🕐 **10am-7.30pm**

*Future champions: Causeway Bay*

### Wise Mount Sports Co **(2, B2)**

This is a long-standing family-run shop with camping gear, swimming goggles, pocketknives, compasses, hard-wearing bags and even sports trophies.

✉ **49 Hankow Rd, Tsim Sha Tsui** ☎ **2787 3011**
🚇 **Tsim Sha Tsui**
🕐 **noon-10pm**

### World Top **(4, F6)**

This smallish shop is crammed with 18-holes worth of golf gear plus a bonus round of tennis racquets.

✉ **Shop 212, Galleria, 9 Queen's Rd Central** ☎ **2521 3703**
🚇 **Central** 🚌 **yes**
🕐 **Mon-Sat 9.30am-6.45pm, Sun 10am-6pm**

### Zoom **(2, B2)**

Superfly treads rule in this teasing strip of sports-shoe shops. All brands and breeds of sneakers get air, get swoosh and get going here. It's packed on weekends.

✉ **65 Fa Yuen St, Mong Kok (p. 47)**
☎ **2781 0920**
🚇 **Mong Kok**
🕐 **11.30am-11pm**

# ANTIQUES & FURNISHINGS

### Arch Angel Antiques

**(6, B2)** Though the specialities are antique and ancient porcelain and tombware, Arch Angel packs a lot more into its three floors: there's everything from mah jong sets to terracotta horses to palatial furniture. You'll feel as comfortable here buying a small gift as a feature ornament for the salon.

✉ **53-55 Hollywood Rd, Central** ☎ **2851 6828** 🚇 **Central, Sheung Wan** 🚌 **26**
🕐 **9.30am-6.30pm**

### Caravan **(6, B2)**

Trustworthy rug-sellers

travel all over Asia to stock this nicely cluttered shop. The range of Afghan and Tibetan carpets is especially notable among a varied rug range.

✉ **65 Hollywood Rd, Central** ☎ **2547 3821**
🚇 **Central, Sheung Wan** 🚌 **26**
🕐 **10am-7pm**

### Chine Gallery **(6, C3)**

Carefully restored furniture (we love the lacquered cabinets) from all over China and hand-knotted rugs from remote regions like Xinjiang, Ningxia, Gansu and Inner Mongolia. All items are sourced by

two brothers, Zafar and Anwer Islam, who own the shop and oversee the restoration.

✉ **42a Hollywood Rd, Central** ☎ **2543 0023**
🚇 **Central, Sheung Wan** 🚌 **26** 🕐 **Mon-Sat 10am-7pm, Sun 1-6pm**

### Chinese Carpet Centre Ltd **(3, J2)**

You'll be floored by the huge selection of new carpets and rugs, most of them made in China but some from as far away as France.

✉ **Shop 168, Ocean Terminal, Canton Rd, Tsim Sha Tsui**

☎ 2735 1030
🚇 Tsim Sha Tsui
🕐 10am-7pm

**Hobbs & Bishops Fine Art** (6, C3)
Waxy-smelling shop specialising in lacquered wooden furniture from 19th-century northern China. Their eye tends more to sleekly handsome than ostentatious pieces.
✉ 28 Hollywood Rd, Central ☎ 2537 9838
🚇 Central 🚌 26
🕐 Mon-Sat 10am-6pm

**Karin Weber Antiques** (6, C2)
An enjoyable mix of Chinese country antiques and contemporary Asian artworks. The folk here give short lectures on antiques and the scene in Hong Kong and provide shopping services for serious, focused buyers.
✉ 32a Staunton St, Soho ☎ 2544 5004
🚇 Central, Sheung Wan 🕐 Mon-Sat 11am-7pm

**Mir Oriental Carpets** (6, D4) This place has wall-to-wall-to-ceiling carpets mostly from Iran. The antique carpets are exquisite and expensive; the new carpets warp and weft from repro to hip.
✉ New India House, 52 Wyndham St, Central ☎ 2521 5641
🚇 Central 🚌 26
🕐 Mon-Sat 10am-7pm, Sun 11am-5pm

**Schoeni Fine Oriental Art** (6, C3)
This Swiss company has been in Hong Kong for over 20 years. It specialises in 17th- to 19th-century Chinese antique furniture

> ## Traditional Medicine
> The Chinese have been using traditional medicine for over three millennia. Concoctions can include fungi, buds, seeds and roots, or the more ghoulish deer antlers, snake blood and bear's bile. It's enough to make you feel well.
>
> **Eu Yan Sang** (6, A3; ☎ 2544 3870), 152-156 Queens Rd, Central, may not be able to diagnose, but its stock is labelled in English so you can be sure you're getting the rhino horn you're after (yes, be warned that endangered animals sometimes fall victim to the medicinal realm). And you know you're in Hong Kong when you see a medicinal herb shop with a sign stating: CLEARANCE SALE EVERYTHING MUST GO!

and Southeast Asian ceramics.
✉ Hollywood House, 27 Hollywood Rd, Central ☎ 2542 3143
🚇 Central 🕐 Mon-Sat 10am-6pm

**Tai Sing Company** (6, D4) Tai Sing has been selling quality Chinese antiques for 50 years with a special focus on porcelain. Two of the shop's six floors are now devoted to European furniture, including a dandy assembly of Art Deco pieces.
✉ 12 Wyndham St, Central ☎ 2525 9365
🚇 Central 🕐 Mon-Sat 10am-6pm

**Tibetan Gallery** (6, D4) This small showroom heads a string of antique and reproduction shops in the building. In this one you'll find Tibetan artefacts from rugs to mini-altars.
✉ Yu Yuet Lai Bldg, 55 Wyndham St, Central ☎ 2530 4863
🚇 Central 🚌 26
🕐 Mon-Sat 10.30am-7.30pm, Sun noon-6pm

*Prewar poster art: a staple in Hong Kong's markets*

# SOUVENIRS & GIFTS

**Alan Chan Creations**
(3, J4) Alan Chan has designed everything from airport logos to soy sauce bottles, and he now lends his name to stylish souvenirs such as clothes and ceramics. Some he has a hand in, others he simply approves of.
✉ **Shop 5a, The Peninsula, cnr Salisbury & Nathan Rds, Tsim Sha Tsui** ☎ **2723 2722**
🚇 **Tsim Sha Tsui**
🕐 **Mon-Sat 10am-7pm**

**Chinese Arts & Crafts**
(3, J3) An Aladdin's department store of souvenirs. Carpets, silks, model boats, you name it… Also at 59 Queen's Rd Central, Central (6, B5); and Pacific Place, Admiralty (4, G9).
✉ **Star House, 3 Salisbury Rd, Tsim Sha Tsui** ☎ **2735 4061**
🚇 **Tsim Sha Tsui**
🕐 **10am-9.30pm**

**Design Gallery**
(4, D12) Supported by the Hong Kong Trade Development Council, this shop showcases local design in the form of jewellery, toys, ornaments and gadgets. It's a some-what chaotic – but often rewarding – gaggle of goodies.
✉ **Hong Kong Convention & Exhibition Centre, 1 Harbour Rd, Wan Chai** ☎ **2584 4146** 🚇 **Wan Chai**
🕐 **10am-7pm**

**King & Country** (4, G9)
This place has models and miniatures, mostly of a military bent (the American War of Independence, and

so forth). There are also street models of old Hong Kong: building frontages, a Chinese wedding proces-sion, even an 'amah' (maid) with baby and chicken'.
✉ **Shop 362, Pacific Place, 88 Queensway, Admiralty** ☎ **2525 8603** 🚇 **Admiralty**
🚻 **yes** 🕐 **Mon-Sat 10.30am-8pm, Sun noon-6pm**

**Liuligongfang** (4, E5)
Exquisite coloured objects, both practical (glasses, bowls, vases and candle holders) and ornamental (figurines, crystal Buddhas, breathtaking sculptures) can be found in abundance here. Everything comes from the one design studio and workshop in China.
✉ **Shop 20-22, Central Bldg, 1-3 Pedder St, Central** ☎ **2973 0820**
🚇 **Central** 🚻 **yes**
🕐 **10am-7.30pm**

**Mandarin Oriental Flower & Gift Shop**
(4, E6) Crockery, cushion covers, chopsticks, tasteful souvenirs and a small selection of jewellery will appeal whether you're looking for gifts or treats for yourself.
✉ **Shop 13-14, Mandarin Oriental Hotel, 5 Connaught Rd, Central** ☎ **2840 1974**
🚇 **Central** 🕐 **Mon-Fri 9am-7pm, Sat 9am-6pm, Sun 10am-5pm**

**Mountain Folkcraft**
(6, C5) One of the nicest shops in town for folk crafts. This place has batik, clothing, woodcarvings and lacquerware made by Asian

ethnic minorities. The shop attendants are friendly, and prices, while not cheap, are not outrageous either.
✉ **12 Wo On Lane, Lan Kwai Fong** ☎ **2525 3199** 🚇 **Central** 🚌 **13, 26, 43** 🕐 **Mon-Sat 9.30am-6.30pm**

**Stone Village** (2, B2)
Creative plant pots, pottery figurines and tea sets plus a lot of beautiful bonsai that you're unfortunately unlikely to be able to take home.
✉ **44 Flower Market Rd, Mong Kok (p. 47)** ☎ **2787 0218**
🚇 **Prince Edward** 🚌 **1, 1A, 2C, 12A** 🕐 **9.30am-7.30pm**

**Yue Hwa** (3, F5)
There are five Yue Hwa shops in Hong Kong, but this is the brightest and biggest. It's one-stop shop-ping Chinese style: bolts of silk, herbs, clothes, porcel-ain, luggage, umbrellas, kitchenware – it's all here.
✉ **Park Lane, 143-161 Nathan Rd, Tsim Sha Tsui** ☎ **2739 3888**
🚇 **Jordan, Tsim Sha Tsui** 🕐 **10am-10pm**

---

## Street-side Souvenirs

If you're 'in the market' for souvenirs, head to one of the following: **Cat St Market** (4, C2; p. 40), **Jade Market** (3, B3; p. 40), **Stanley Market** (2, E4; p. 40), **Western Market** (4, B2; p. 40) or **Temple St Night Market** (p. 26).

# places to eat

There's a saying that the only four-legged thing a Cantonese person won't eat is a table. Observation suggests that the only flying object deemed inedible is an aeroplane and anything underwater is fair game unless it's wearing a swimsuit. This collective passion for eating makes Hong Kong one of the world's great foodie cities – grab your chopsticks and tuck in.

## Cuisines

Most of Hong Kong's 10,000 restaurants are Chinese. Cantonese is the home-town cuisine but Chiu Chow and Shanghainese food is also easy to find. Cantonese cuisine is famously fresh: there's an emphasis on fresh-killed meat, mostly pork and seafood. Simple techniques like steaming and stir-frying allow the ingredients to shine. Chiu Chow food makes liberal use of garlic, vinegar and sauces; it's famous for cold goose, crab and other delicacies. Shanghainese cooking uses a lot more salted and preserved foods and depends on stewing, braising and frying. Dumplings and noodles are often eaten instead of rice. Don't fear if a tasty-looking restaurant doesn't have English signage; many places have an English menu tucked away somewhere.

And don't worry if you're having a bad noodle day. Hong Kong is where East eats West and you're liable to see bangers 'n' mash, lasagne and *croque-monsieur* before there's time to say 'beef tendon congee'. The highest concentration of Western restaurants is in Soho and Lan Kwai Fong. Every neighbourhood is studded with cheap and mid-range Chinese restaurants – take a turn off the main streets to find plenty of bustling noodle bars. The top Chinese restaurants are in hotels – there's no shame in heading to a hotel restaurant for a special meal.

### Price Ranges

For cheap eats in Hong Kong follow the locals into soup and noodle restaurants. More sophisticated Chinese, other Asian and Western restaurants are usually more pricey. Keep in mind that many restaurants have value-priced set lunches. However, beware that straying from the menu will most likely incur a cost – especially at top-end restaurants, where a bottle of water can add $40 to the bill.

The price scale below represents the cost of an average dinner with a glass of wine.

| | |
|---|---|
| $ | under $50 |
| $$ | $51-149 |
| $$$ | $150-350 |
| $$$$ | over $350 |

*Forget about menus, just point*

## Etiquette

Eating out is usually a casual affair but there are a few points of etiquette it doesn't hurt to keep in mind. Top-end restaurants require smart casual dress: sports shoes and shorts may not be acceptable. Men can forego a tie – a collared shirt will suffice.

### At the Table

- Dining in Hong Kong is an all-in affair: everyone shares dishes, chats loudly and makes a mess
- Food is to be enjoyed wholeheartedly, not picked at discreetly
- Do wait until others start before digging in (but as a guest you may well be asked to start)
- Don't reach for tasty morsels from the far side of dishes – what's closest to you is yours
- Do say thanks if someone puts food into your bowl – this is a very kind and courteous gesture
- Do make a mess – a stained tablecloth is a sign of a good meal
- Do answer your mobile phone at anytime during the meal
- Do cover your mouth when using a toothpick
- Don't try to clean up dishes and detritus – why destroy the evidence?

## Drinks

The typical liquid accompaniment to Chinese food is tea – it's drunk from the meal's beginning to end from a periodically refilled pot. Beer is available almost everywhere but wine doesn't start to feature until you're in mid- to upper-range places. Top Chinese restaurants pay great attention to their wine lists but the mark-ups are savage. Western restaurants tend to have small, unexciting lists with a couple of reasonable tipples available by the glass.

## Booking & Tipping

In all but the cheapies, it's advisable to book ahead, especially on Friday and Saturday nights. Most restaurants add a 10% service charge. In cheap to mid-range restaurants, you can consider this a tip. In expensive restaurants, it's assumed you'll tip up to 10% on top of the service charge.

### Kid-Friendly Kitchens

Children are generally welcome in Hong Kong's restaurants – we've indicated the ones that are particularly family friendly (look for the ☺ in reviews). Hardly any restaurants have highchairs or booster seats so bring your own if you can't do without. Though most restaurants don't do special children's serves, Chinese food lends itself to sharing and it's easy to create your own munchkin-sized portions.

# Hoorah for Yum Cha!

Yum cha (literally 'to drink tea') is the usual way to refer to dim sum, the unique-ly Cantonese snacks that are served for breakfast or lunch (usually between about 7am and 2pm). Eating dim sum is a social occasion, consisting of many separate dishes which are meant to be shared. The bigger your group the better!

Dim sum delicacies are normally steamed in small bamboo baskets. In most dim sum restaurants you order from a menu but in older-style places the baskets are stacked up on pushcarts and rolled around the dining room. Just stop the waiter and choose something from the cart. Don't worry about trying everything you're offered: each pushcart has a different selection, so stagger your selections to give your stomach a fair go. It's estimated there are about 1000 dim sum dishes – you'd be doing very well to sample 10 in one sitting.

Dim sum restaurants can be so large that the servers use walkie-talkies to communicate with the kitchen. They get very crowded, especially at lunch time and even more so on weekends. There's a friendly, fun buzz as the groups, often extended families, talk loudly and share food and tea.

The 10th floor of Times Square shopping centre in Causeway Bay (5, G2) holds a couple of restaurants doing a roaring trade. Choose between **Heichinrou** (☎ 2506 2333; $$), the most elegant place up here, and **King Palace** (☎ 2506 3939; $$). Other dim sum destinations include **City Hall Chinese Restaurant** (p. 72), **Yung Kee** (p. 73), **Zen** (p. 73), **Lin Heung Tea House** (p. 76), **Chinese Restaurant** (p. 81), **Sweet Dynasty** (p. 82), **Wan Loong Court** (p. 83), **Dynasty** (p. 85) and **Super Star Seafood Restaurant** (p. 86).

Dim sum dishes include:
*cha siu bau* – barbecued pork buns
*cheung fan* – steamed rice-flour rolls with shrimp, beef or pork
*ching chau sichoi* – fried green vegetable of the day
*chun guen* – fried spring rolls
*fan gwo* – steamed dumplings with pork, shrimp and bamboo shoots
*fung jau* – fried chicken's feet
*gaisi chaumin* – fried crispy noodles with shredded chicken
*gon siu yimin* – dry-fried noodles
*ha gau* – shrimp dumplings
*ham sui gok* – fried rice-flour triangles (usually with pork inside)
*ho yip fan* – rice wrapped in lotus leaf
*pai gwat* – steamed spare ribs
*san juk ngau yok* – steamed minced-beef balls
*siu mai* – pork and shrimp dumplings
*woo gok* – deep-fried taro puffs

# ADMIRALTY & CENTRAL

## City Hall Chinese Restaurant
(4, E7) **$$**

*Chinese, Cantonese*
This crazily busy dim sum restaurant has great harbour views but everyone's too busy eating to gaze outside. The dim sum comes by on wheelie carts and the morsels are adequately explained by the servers. Arrive before noon if you want to avoid queuing with office groups and wedding parties.
✉ **Low Block, City Hall, 7 Edinburgh Pl** ☎ 2521 1303 🚇 Central ⏰ 10am-3pm, 5.30-11pm ♨

## Refills & Respect

If your teapot is running empty, let the waiter know by taking the lid off the pot. The story behind this custom tells of a diner who decided to keep his prize pigeon warm in the empty teapot. When the waiter refilled the pot he boiled the bird.

If you wish to thank the waiter but your mouth is full, tap the table with three fingers. The middle finger represents a bowed head and the other fingers prostrate arms.

## Dai Pai Dong (6, A3) **$**

*Chinese, Hong Kong Snacks*
This modern version of the outdoor snack stand serves breakfast (bacon and eggs, porridge, instant noodles), lunch and dinner (noodles) but it's best to come at afternoon tea for *yuan yang* (half-tea, half-coffee), and toast smeared with condensed milk. Also at 70 Canton Rd, Tsim Sha Tsui (3, G3); and 20 Russell St, Causeway Bay (5, F2).
✉ **128 Queen's Rd Central** ☎ 2851 6389 🚇 Central ⏰ Mon-Sat 8am-10pm, Sun 9.30am-7pm (afternoon tea: 2.30-5.30pm) ♨ Ⓥ

## Eating Plus (4, D6) **$$**

*International*
Style comes cheap at this very vogue eatery and bar. Breakfasts are a snip (around $25) – omelettes are fluffy, juices are freshly squeezed. Lunch and dinner extend to soups, noodles (East and West) and risotto; reasonable set meals are available. Great health juices too.
✉ **Shop 1009, IFC Mall, 1 Harbour View St** ☎ 2868 0599 🚇 Central ⏰ Mon-Sat 7.30am-10pm, Sun 7.30am-8pm ♨ Ⓥ

## Hunan Garden (4, D5) **$$$**

*Chinese, Hunanese*
This elegant place specialises in spicy Hunanese cuisine. The fried chicken with chilli is excellent, as are the seafood dishes. Views, overlooking the harbour or the heart of Central, are a bonus.
✉ **Forum Mall,**

Exchange Sq, 8 Connaught Pl ☎ 2868 2880 🚇 Central ⏰ 11.30am-3pm, 5.30-11.30pm Ⓥ

## Luk Yu Tea House
(6, C5) **$$$**

*Chinese*
Long-standing Luk Yu is a popular dim sum venue. It became an institution because of its delicate dishes, now it's just an institution, stalked by grouchy elderly waiters. The booths are uncomfortable, it's not cheap, prices aren't marked…yes, things have changed at Luk Yu.
✉ **24-26 Stanley St** ☎ 2523 5464 🚇 Central ⏰ 7am-10pm (dim sum until 5pm) ♨

## Mix (4, F6) **$**

*International*
A good, no-nonsense spot to grab a meal on the fly, or munch while surfing the in-house Internet. Points deducted for meal names – *you* try ordering a 'beef injection' while keeping a straight face. Also in the IFC Mall, Central (4, D6).
✉ **Shop 11, Standard Chartered Bank Bldg, 3 Queen's Rd Central** ☎ 2523 7396 ⏰ Mon-Sat 7am-8pm, Sun 9am-6pm ♨ Ⓥ

## Mughal Room
(6, D4) **$$**

*Indian*
Recommended Mughal Room dishes include the superb samosas, the *dahi papri* (lentil crisps covered with tamarind-yoghurt sauce) and the *paneer dilbahar* (cream cheese and potato balls stuffed with dried fruit). The lunch

buffet is excellent value.
✉ **Carfield Commercial Bldg, 75-77 Wyndham St** ☎ 2524 0107
Ⓔ Central Ⓒ noon-3pm, 6-11pm **V**

### Nicholini's (4, G9) $$$$
*Italian*

This refined restaurant's approach to northern Italian cuisine has won it praise from Italian expatriates and even an *Insegna Del Ristorante Italiano* (Best Italian Restaurant – abroad) by the President of Italy. Simple yet superb antipasto as well as shellfish dishes are just a few firm Nicholini favourites.
✉ **8th fl, Conrad International, 88 Queensway** ☎ 2521 3838 Ⓔ Admiralty
Ⓒ 11.30am-3.30pm, 6.30-11pm

### The Square (4, D6) $$$
*Cantonese*

This slick newcomer made a splash with stylish reworkings of Cantonese favourites. The hushed atmosphere and dedicated service make it a good choice for business or romance.
✉ **Exchange Sq, 8 Connaught Pl** ☎ 2525 1163 Ⓔ Central
Ⓒ 11am-3pm, 6-11pm

### Thai Basil (4, G9) $$$
*Thai*

The chaos of Pacific Place dissolves when you enter Thai Basil, replaced with a laid-back atmosphere and the lure of green curries and other Thai classics. Other parts of Indochina make their way onto the menu, including Vietnamese rice-paper rolls. Leave room for a cardamom or mango-chilli sorbet.
✉ **Shop 005, Pacific**

*Mix on Queen's Rd, Central*

**Place, 88 Queensway** ☎ 2537 4682
Ⓔ Admiralty
Ⓒ 11.30am-3.30pm, 6-11pm

### Vong (4, E6)    $$$$
*French, Southeast Asian*

Dramatic Vong features a creative mix of Vietnamese, French and Thai food. Consider the tasting menu ($500) to get a full appreciation of the combination of French techniques with Asian flavours. Herbivores will appreciate the extensive vegetarian menu.
✉ **Mandarin Oriental Hotel, 5 Connaught Rd** ☎ 2825 4028
Ⓔ Central Ⓒ noon-3pm, 6pm-midnight (bar until 2am) **V**

### Yè Shanghai (4, G9)    $$$
*Chinese, Shanghainese*

A newish player that takes street-level Shanghai cuisine and gives it a tweak here and there. The drunken pigeon is a wine-soaked winner and the steamed dumplings are perfectly plump, but sometimes this restaurant goes for clattery style over substance.
✉ **Shop 332, Pacific Place, 88 Queensway** ☎ 2918 9833

Ⓔ Admiralty
Ⓒ 11.30am-3pm, 6-11.30pm **V**

### Yung Kee (6, C5) $$$
*Chinese*

This is Hong Kong's reigning patriarch of Cantonese restaurants. The roast goose here has been the talk of the town since 1942 (it farms its own geese for quality control), and its dim sum is also excellent. Yung Kee may have retired, but he still lurks, approving menu changes and keeping the army of staff on their toes.
✉ **32-40 Wellington St** ☎ 2522 0631
Ⓔ Central Ⓒ 11am-11.30pm

### Zen (4, G9)    $$$$
*Chinese*

Cantonese and Shanghainese dishes in a Japanese interior. Zen has won praise from the public and restaurateurs alike for its dynamic approach to Chinese cuisine. You'll enjoy mangoes with your prawns and a multitude of dim sum dishes. Private rooms are available.
✉ **LG1, The Mall, Pacific Place, 88 Queensway** ☎ 2845 4555 Ⓔ Admiralty
Ⓒ 11.30am-3.30pm

# LAN KWAI FONG

**Beirut** (6, D5) $$$
*Lebanese*
A faux tavern where you can snack on hummus and bread washed down with beer or settle in for a whole sheep. The mixed grills are smoky and juicy and the service is pretty handy for such a bustling place.
✉ **Winner Bldg, 27-39 D'Aguilar St** ☎ **2804 6611** Ⓔ Central
🕐 noon-12.30am **V**

**China Lan Kwai Fong** (6, D5) $$$
*Chinese*
China's menu is as broad as its name suggests, but the menu alludes to which part of the mainland your drunken pork heralds from (Zhejiang). Inside it's oriental elegance thick with wood and silk, making it perfect for a quiet business lunch or romantic evening.
✉ **17-22 Lan Kwai Fong** ☎ **2536 0968** Ⓔ Central 🕐 noon-3pm, 6.30-11pm

**Chop Chop Café** (6, D5) $
*American, International*
The Chop Chop is a small, cheap eatery where you can fill up on baked potatoes, casseroles and other speedy cuisine. There are three

good reasons to come here: you need beer soaker, you need it now and you need it cheap.
✉ **17 Wing Wah Lane** ☎ **2526 1122** Ⓔ Central 🕐 11.30am-11pm 🔽 **V**

**M at the Fringe** (6, E5) $$$$
*International*
No-one seems to have a bad thing to say about Michelle's. The menu changes constantly, but everything is excellent, whether it's *bachalao* or slow-baked salted lamb. It's worth saving room for dessert, if you have that kind of self-restraint. Set lunches are $150. Reservations are a must.
✉ **South Block, 2 Lwr Albert Rd** ☎ **2877 4000** Ⓔ Central 🕐 Mon-Fri noon-2.30pm, 7-10.30pm **V**

**Taste Good** (6, D5) $$
*Thai, Cantonese*
Upbeat café at the slops end of Lan Kwai Fong's charmingly nicknamed Rat Alley. Simple, filling meat and vegetable curries come hot enough to raise a sweat; there are soups, noodles and more elaborate barbecued

dishes too.
✉ **16 Wing Wah Lane** ☎ **2523 9543** Ⓔ Central 🕐 11am-1am **V**

**Va Bene** (6, D5) $$$
*Italian*
This smart restaurant bears a striking resemblance to a neighbourhood trattoria. Unusually for Hong Kong, the house bread is excellent, but don't fill up before you get to the spaghetti or the lamb's shanks. It's a good choice for a special date or an extravagant celebration. Book ahead; dress smart.
✉ **58-62 D'Aguilar St** ☎ **2845 5577** Ⓔ Central 🕐 noon-3pm, 7pm-midnight

*The sign says it all: elegance at M at the Fringe*

# SOHO

### Bistro Manchu
(6, C2) **$$**
*Manchurian*
Cosy and easy-going place specialising in myriad dumplings with dipping sauce (the cucumber and tofu combo is a vegetarian winner), plus soups and other three-bite snacks such as fried eggplant stuffed with shredded pork. The pleasant dining room is red-themed with original (but not Manchurian) art.
✉ 33 Elgin St ☎ 2536 9218 Ⓗ Central
🕐 noon-2.30pm, 6-11pm **V**

### Blue (6, C3) **$$$**
*International*
Style and substance come together within this

*They've been doing it since Marco Polo: noodles all'Italia*

clinically sleek restaurant. The Australians running this place have imported antipodean flavours such as New Zealand lip mussels with beer, blue vein and pimiento, and an extensive Australian wine list.
✉ 43-45 Lyndhurst Tce ☎ 2815 4005
Ⓗ Central 🕐 noon-3pm, 7.30-11pm **V**

### Boca (6, C2) **$$$**
*Spanish*
This spot goes down well with expats, who sprawl on the lounges and over-order from the tasty tapas menu. A prime locale to watch foot traffic on Elgin St.
✉ 65 Peel St ☎ 2548 1717 Ⓗ Central
🕐 11am-2am **V**

### Cubana (6, D2) **$$$**
*Cuban*
Two-storey Cuban place with a good selection of tapas and serious cocktail pitchers. There's a barnyard of main dishes (pork, chicken, beef) plus a fish dish. The food is good, though a bit heavy for Hong Kong's humid summers, and the service can be tentative.
✉ 47b Elgin St

☎ 2869 1218
Ⓗ Central 🕐 noon-2am (lunch: noon-2pm; dinner: 6pm-midnight)

### DaLuca (6, C3) **$$$**
*Italian*
This slice of Italy under the shade of the escalator serves fresh favourites such as pizza, pasta and antipasto. The familiar food, starch linen and weighty cutlery makes DaLuca a good choice for refined dining.
✉ 46-48 Cochrane St
Ⓗ Central ☎ 2544 6346 🕐 noon-midnight

### India Today (6, C2) **$$**
*Indian*
India Today is a worthy player in the 'How many restaurants can you get on one block?' competition, which has Elgin St in a frenzy. The curries are reasonably priced, the beer is icy and the atmosphere is pleasant.
✉ 1st fl, 26-30 Elgin St ☎ 2801 5959
Ⓗ Central 🕐 noon-3pm, 6-11.30pm **V**

### Le Rendez-vous (6, C3) **$**
*French*
Tiny nautically themed crepe house that also does

## Late-Night Bites
Most restaurants stop serving meals around 11pm but some won't let the chefs go home till the wee hours. Lan Kwai Fong and Soho are good places for nocturnal dining, as are the streets of Yau Ma Tei and Mong Kok (p. 86). Take your insomniac stomach to these late-night spots: **Boca** (p. 75), **Cubana** (p. 75), **Felix** (p. 81), **Global Forever-Green Taiwanese Restaurant** (p. 77), **Good Hope Noodle** (p. 79), **Leung Hing Seafood Restaurant** (p. 80), **Tack Hsin Restaurant** (p. 78) and **369 Shanghai Restaurant** (p. 86).

baguettes and salads. The crepes come filled with classic combos like mushroom and cheese, along with more adventurous spicy inventions. There's a full bar too with a happy hour from 6pm to 8pm.

✉ 5 Staunton St
☎ 2905 1808
Ⓒ Central ⏰ 10am-11.30pm ♿ **V**

### Lin Heung Tea House
(4, D3) $
*Chinese, Cantonese*
Older-style Cantonese restaurant packed with old men reading the newspaper, families and office groups. There's OK dim sum (the food comes around on a trolley and it's a good place to dine alone) but it's also recommended for a bite late at night. It's a very local place, but there's an English menu. Book ahead.

✉ 160-164 Wellington St (cnr Aberdeen St)
☎ 2544 4556
Ⓒ Central
⏰ 6am-11pm ♿

### Orange Tree
(6, D2) $$$
*Dutch*
Modern Dutch food served in a breezy russet setting in

the higher reaches of the escalator. Don't get stuck on the sausages – there are lighter dishes like puff pastries. For dessert there are always *poffertjes* (Dutch pancakes) on the menu.

✉ 17 Shelley St
☎ 2838 9352
Ⓒ Central ⏰ Sat-Sun noon-3pm, daily 6-10.30pm **V**

### Soho Soho
(6, C3) $$$
*British*
Post-colonially, New British food has taken off with *Chuppies* (Chinese yuppies) and Poms on expense accounts. It's creative (crumpet with smoked salmon), homy (roasted cod with new potatoes) and manly (chump of lamb with a pepper crust). Desserts are pure Brit treats like treacle tart and clotted cream.

✉ 9 Old Bailey St
☎ 2147 2618
Ⓒ Central ⏰ Mon-Sat noon-2.30pm, 7-10.30pm

### Two Sardines
(6, D2) $$$
*French*
Independent French bistro

### Dai Pai Dong Gets the Gong
Hong Kong authorities are on a long campaign to clear the streets of *dai pai dong,* the open-air street stalls selling noodles and snacks. New licences are not issued and there are restrictions about passing on current licences. This makes the noodle stands in Soho an endangered species – sit and slurp while you can. Street-side dining, however, is alive and well in Yau Ma Tei and Mong Kok (p. 86).

that deserves the crowds it draws. The namesake fish comes grilled with a zesty sauce; the liver is worth trying too. The wine list leans predictably to the Gallic but is likely to please. Set lunches are excellent value.

✉ 43 Elgin St ☎ 2973 6618 Ⓒ Central
⏰ Mon-Sat noon-3pm, 6.30pm-midnight

### Yi Jiang Nan
(6, C2) $$
*Chinese*
Southern Chinese cuisine served under bird-cage lanterns. Behind the dark wood exterior prevails a subdued, homely atmosphere, although the frescoes are a tad too Tuscan. Meat freaks should order the house speciality: fried pig's throat.

✉ 33-35 Staunton St
☎ 2111 2822
Ⓒ Central ⏰ noon-3pm, 6-10.30pm ♿

*The Lin Heung Tea House: no-fuss dim sum*

# CAUSEWAY BAY

### Chuen Cheung Kui
(5, G2) $$
*Chinese, Hakka*
Enlist a Cantonese dining companion or dive in bravely: there's not much English spoken here and the food is challenging. Gizzard soup and stomach tidbit are two of the less alluring menu items. The pulled chicken, a Hakka classic, is the dish to insist upon.
✉ 110-112 Percival St
☎ 2577 3833
Ⓖ Causeway Bay
🕐 11am-midnight

### Cova Ristorante
(5, G3) $$$
*Italian*
This is as romantic as it gets in the basement of an office block: pastels, twinkling waiters and upholstered chairs. Whether it's pasta or pastries, charge up on a good approximation of Milan's best coffee before heading back to the throng. Also in the Prince's Bldg, Central (4, E6); and Pacific Place, Admiralty (4, G9).
✉ Shop B01, Lee Gardens, 33 Hysan Ave
☎ 2907 3399
Ⓖ Causeway Bay
🕐 Mon-Sat 8.30am-11pm (high tea: 3-6pm), Sun noon-11pm

### Dining Area (5, F3) $$$
*International*
Super groover hang-out with beautifully presented global cuisine: follow your French-onion soup with Indonesian nasi goreng, or swing by for a sweet soufflé. The sleek decor befits the chic clientele.
✉ 17 Lan Fong Rd
☎ 2915 0260
Ⓖ Causeway Bay
🕐 11.30am-11pm ♿ V

### Forum Restaurant
(5, E2) $$$$
*Chinese*
The Forum's abalone dishes have fans spread across the world. What restaurant owner Ah Yat does with these molluscs has earned him praise from the late Deng Xiaoping, membership to Le Club des Chefs des Chefs and the moniker of King of Abalone. Dress smart, skip lunch and savour the flavour.
✉ 485 Lockhart Rd
☎ 2891 2555
Ⓖ Causeway Bay
🕐 11am-11pm

### Genroku Sushi
(5, G2) $$
*Japanese*
Genroku is Hong Kong's most exotic fast-food chain. The sushi tears around on a conveyor belt. The only drawback is the potentially long wait for seats, especially during the manic 1pm to 2pm lunch hour.
✉ cnr Matheson St & Sharp St E ☎ 2889 8889 Ⓖ Causeway Bay
🕐 11.30am-2am ♿

### Global Forever-Green Taiwanese Restaurant (5, G3) $$
*Taiwanese*
Forever Green is the best place in town for Taiwanese food. Try traditional specialities such as oyster omelette, fried bean curd and sanbeiji (three-cup chicken). Noodle dishes are definitely the best value. There's a pictorial menu to help out novices.
✉ 93-95a Leighton Rd (enter from Sun Wui Rd) ☎ 2890 3448

Ⓖ Causeway Bay
🕐 6pm-4am ♿ V

### Gogo Cafe (5, H3) $$
*Japanese, Italian*
This is where East meets West for spaghetti with mentaiko (fish roe) or rice with home-made bolognaise. The theme here is part Japanese teahouse, part cool café, and the light meals and easy pace make Gogo a good place to re-energise between lunch and dinner.
✉ 11 Caroline Hill Rd
☎ 2881 5598 Ⓖ Causeway Bay 🕐 Mon-Sat noon-11pm ♿ V

## Coffee Concerns
Coffee in Hong Kong tends to be overpriced and of dubious quality (Hong Kong water doesn't help). Nevertheless there are plenty of cafés catering to your caffeine urges, including **Starz Cafe** (6, B3; ☎ 2541 1826), 41-43 Graham St, Soho; **? Coffee Shop** (6, C3; ☎ 2581 2128), 45 Cochrane St, Central; and **Sharp 15** (p. 78). Expensive chain-coffee is available from **Pacific Coffee Company**, **Delifrance** and **Starbucks** in just about every shopping centre. For cheap no-frills coffee look for small Chinese restaurants with a Coca-Cola sign out front – coffee as bad as anywhere for a third of the price.

## Hello Kitty Café
(5, E3)                    $

*Japanese, Snacks*

Cute food like toasties, waffles and sundaes along with more substantial Japanese soup noodles and dumplings. The decor is pink, the waitresses wear black – go figure. Great choice for kids.

✉ Shop 11, 1st fl, Chee On Bldg, 24 East Point Rd (cnr Lockhart Rd) ☎ 2890 9021
🚇 Causeway Bay
🕐 10am-11pm ♿ V

## Heng Fa Low (5, G2) $

*Chinese*

This dessert hotspot has been in the neighbourhood for half a century. People crowd in here until late at night filling up on fruit and jelly concoctions. We're told that *hasma* is frog's sperm soup.

✉ Po Ming Bldg, 49-57 Lee Garden Rd ☎ 2915 7797 🚇 Causeway Bay
🕐 11am-midnight V

## Moon Garden Tea House (5, G3)            $$

*Chinese*

The simple cuppa reaches nirvanic heights at Moon Garden. Choose from many brews then lose an after-

*Moon Garden Tea House*

noon perusing tea books, admiring antiques, snacking on meticulous morsels and taking refills from the heated pot beside your table. Also at 149 Hollywood Rd, Central (4, D2).

✉ 5 Hoi Ping Rd
☎ 2882 6878
🚇 Causeway Bay
🕐 noon-midnight

## Queen's Cafe
(5, G3)                   $$

*Russian*

This smallish Russian café has been here since 1952, accounting for its subdued yet assured atmosphere. The borsch and meat sets are pretty good. Head for nearby **Queen's Cake Shop** (15 Pak Sha Rd) for post-meal cakes and buns.

✉ Eton Tower, 8 Hysan Ave ☎ 2576 2658 🚇 Causeway Bay
🕐 noon-10pm

## Red Pepper (5, F3) $$$

*Chinese, Sichuanese*

If you want to set your palate aflame, try this friendly, long-established restaurant's Sichuanese-style sliced pork in chilli sauce, accompanied by *dan dan mian* (noodles in a spicy peanut soup). Also good are the deep-fried beans and sizzling prawns.

✉ 7 Lan Fong Rd
☎ 2577 3811
🚇 Causeway Bay
🕐 11.30am-midnight

## Sharp 15 (5, G2)       $

*International*

A wide range of brews makes Sharp 15 the place for a caffeine fix, and you can surf the net for free while you clasp your cuppa.

✉ 15 Sharp St E
☎ 2891 9555
🚇 Causeway Bay
🕐 Mon-Thurs

noon-1am, Fri-Sat noon-2am, Sun 3-11pm V

## The Stonegrill
(5, G3)                  $$$

*International*

Don't complain when your food arrives half-cooked – it's supposed to. Steak or fish arrives sunny-side up and sizzling on a slab of stone; you turn it over to taste. It's one of the trendiest restaurants in town so book ahead. Also in Harbour City, Tsim Sha Tsui (3, H3).

✉ 1 Hoi Ping Rd
☎ 2576 1331
🚇 Causeway Bay
🕐 noon-3pm, 6.30pm-1am

## Tack Hsin Restaurant
(5, F4)                  $$$

*Chinese*

Massive restaurant occupied by loud families plunging food into sizzling hotpots. Beware of the prawns: they arrive alive and squirming. The English menu is limited – the deluxe hotpot is a good bet and for breakfast there's tasty dim sum.

✉ 1-13 Sugar St
☎ 2894 8899
🚇 Causeway Bay
🕐 7.30am-1am ♿

## WasabiSabi
(5, G2)                  $$$

*Japanese*

Excellent Japanese cuisine, impeccable service...we've gotta cut to the chase: the interior of this restaurant is bezerk. From cable vines, through to rondo lounges and into the sweeping sushi bar. Even the faux birch forest behind the bar has gumption.

✉ L13, Times Square, 1 Matheson St ☎ 2506 0009 🚇 Causeway Bay
🕐 noon-3pm, 6pm-midnight

# MONG KOK

### Good Hope Noodle
(2, B2)                                  $

*Chinese, Noodles*

This busy noodle-stop is known far and wide for its terrific wonton soups and shredded pork noodles with spicy bean sauce. Good Hope is an eat-and-go sort of place – don't come here if you feel like slurping slowly and lingering.

✉ 146 Sai Yeung Choi St Sth (sth of Mong Kok Rd; p. 47)
☎ 2394 5967
Ⓜ Mong Kok
◷ noon-1am ♿

### Saint's Alp Teahouse
(2, B2)                                  $

*Snacks, Taiwanese*

One in a chain of clean, cheap snackeries in Hong Kong (look for the footprint sign). It's a great pit stop for Taiwanese-style frothy tea with tapioca drops and Chinese snacks like toast with condensed milk, shrimp balls, noodles and rice puddings.

✉ 61a Shantung St (p. 47) ☎ 2782 1438
Ⓜ Mong Kok ◷ Sun-Thurs 10am-11pm, Fri-Sat 10am-midnight
♿ Ⓥ

*Soups & noodles, Mong Kok*

# NEW TERRITORIES

### Cafe Aficionado
(1, E2)                                $$$

*International*

If you've got time to kill at the airport, this large cafeteria/restaurant is a good option. There are buffets for both breakfast and lunch as well as a large all-day menu of Eastern and Western snacks and meals. The burgers are fantastic. Don't bother walking round to admire the art: it's on conveyor belts and comes to you.

✉ Regal Airport Hotel, 9 Cheong Tat Rd, Lantau Is ☎ 2286 8888 (ext 6238) ◷ 24hrs ♿
Ⓥ

### Chuen Kee Seafood Restaurant
(1, D8)                              $$$$

*Chinese, Cantonese, Seafood*

See that queue of fidgety plastic basins that ends at the kitchen? That's dinner. Start by choosing your live seafood from the stall outside, tell the waiters how you'd like it cooked and then wait for it to progress, flipping and flap-ping to the kitchen. Most people eating at this no-frills restaurant order their catch steamed and simple.

✉ 51-55 Hoi Pong St (on the waterfront), Sai Kung ☎ 2791 1195
Ⓜ Choi Hung (then bus 92 or minibus 1, 1A, 4)
◷ 11am-11pm ♿

### Federal Restaurant
(2, B3)                                  $$

*Chinese, Cantonese*

This is a bustling restaurant (not Federal Seafood) so big that the waiters have walkie-talkies. Dim sum is served until mid-afternoon and Cantonese à la carte at dinner. The dim sum menu is in Chinese only – ask your waiter to choose for you or stickybeak at other tables and point. Feature windows look out onto a very Hong Kong vista of apartments; the MTR station is right downstairs.

✉ 3rd fl, Hollywood Plaza, 3 Lung Poon St, Diamond Hill ☎ 2626 0011 Ⓜ Diamond Hill
◷ 7.30am-11pm ♿

### Jaspa's (1, D8)                 $$$

*European*

Multi-ethnic Jaspa's in Sai Kung attracts groups of expats who can't bear to face another round with chopsticks, as well as trendy locals dining on tasty pasta, stir-fries and steaks. There's also an excellent, extensive vegetarian selection. The atmosphere is rollicking Mediterranean.

✉ 13 Sha Tsui Path (opp the playground), Sai Kung ☎ 2792 6388
Ⓜ Choi Hung (then bus 92 or minibus 1)
◷ Mon-Sat 10am-10.30pm, Sun 9.30am-10pm ♿ Ⓥ

# SHEUNG WAN

### Korea Garden
(4, C3)                    $$$
*Korean*
This comfortable restaurant serves a delicious array of appetisers (dried fish, salad, pickles, chillied cabbage leaves, spring rolls) which come as side dishes to BBQ dishes (sizzled at your table), *kimchi* pancakes, grilled fish and ground meat in egg batter.
✉ **Blissful Bldg, 247 Des Voeux Rd Central**
☎ **2542 2339**
🚇 **Sheung Wan**
🕐 **11am-11.30pm** **V**

### Leung Hing Seafood Restaurant
(4, C1)                    $$
*Chinese, Chiu Chow*
The Chiu Chow region's primary cooking ingredients – seafood, goose and duck – are extensively employed and delectably prepared at Leung Hing Seafood Restaurant. Try the classic soyed goose and then revel in the lip-smacking desserts.
✉ **32 Bonham Strand W**
☎ **2850 6666**
🚇 **Sheung Wan**
🕐 **noon-2am** ♨

*Anyone for rice wine?*

# SOUTHERN HONG KONG ISLAND

### The Boathouse
(2, E4)                    $$$
*International*
All aboard for nautical overload. Salads, bruschetta and Med-inspired mains make up the bulk of The Boathouse's fleet. Aim for sea views. Spinnaker's Bar serves snacks all day.
✉ **86-88 Stanley Main St** ☎ **2813 4467** 🚌 **6, 66, 262** 🕐 **10.30am-midnight** **V**

### El Cid Caramar
(2, E4)                    $$
*Spanish*
El Cid Caramar in historic Murray House (p. 49) serves a good range of tapas, and with the harbour view and too many *cervezas* you'll think you're in San Sebastian. Also at 12-14 Knutsford Tce, Tsim Sha Tsui (3, F6).
✉ **Shop 102, Murray House, Stanley Plaza**
☎ **2899 0858** 🚌 **6, 66, 262** 🕐 **11am-10.30pm** ♨ **V**

### Jumbo Floating Restaurant
(2, D2) $$$
*Chinese*
Floating restaurants have made Aberdeen world famous. Jumbo's interior looks like Beijing's Imperial Palace crossbred with a Las Vegas casino. It's not so much a restaurant as an institution. That's how diners should view it, since the overpriced food leaves something to be desired. Transport to and from the restaurant is via boats, which run between piers at the Aberdeen Promenade and next to the Aberdeen Marina Club.
✉ **Aberdeen Marina**
☎ **2873 7111** 🚌 **70, 75** 🕐 **Mon-Sat 11am-11pm, Sun 7am-11pm** ♨

### Lucy's (2, E4)        $$$
*Continental*
Easy-going place that doesn't overwhelm with choice but with just how good the food is. The menu changes frequently as fresh produce

and inspiration strikes, but the offerings tend to honest fusion rather than fancy flim-flammery. There's a good selection of wines by the glass.
✉ **64 Stanley Main St (in the market)**
☎ **2813 9055** 🚌 **6, 66, 262** 🕐 **noon-3pm, 7-10pm** **V**

### The Verandah
(2, D3)                  $$$$
*Continental, Asian*
In the new-colonial bit of the wavy Repulse Bay condos, The Verandah is hushed and formal with heavy white tablecloths and demurely clinking cutlery. The brunch is famous (book way ahead and dream about the caviar-topped eggs benedict); the afternoon tea is the south side's best.
✉ **The Repulse Bay, 109 Repulse Bay Rd**
☎ **2812 2722** 🚌 **61** 🕐 **noon-2.30pm, 6.30-11pm**

# TSIM SHA TSUI

### Chinese Restaurant (3, H4)    $$$$
*Chinese*
It may not win any awards for its name, but the Chinese Restaurant has a solid reputation for its seasonal menu and dim sum. If you order the Peking duck you'll get a numbered certificate, linking you to the bird forever. Solo diners will appreciate the set menu for one.
✉ **Hyatt Regency Hotel, 67 Nathan Rd** ☎ 2311 1234 (ext 2881) ◉ Tsim Sha Tsui ◷ 11.30am-3pm, 6.30-11pm ♿ V

### Dong (3, F5)    $$$
*Chinese*
It's the classic hotel restaurant interior right down to the chintzy music, but Dong's menu does offer an authentically adventurous twist with seafood soups and a forest of fungus. A good choice if you want to keep the cultural experience limited to the plate.
✉ **Arcade 2, Hotel Miramar, 118-130 Nathan Rd** ☎ 2315 5166 ◉ Tsim Sha Tsui ◷ 11am-3pm, 6-10.30pm V

### Felix (3, J5)    $$$$
*International*
Felix has a fantastic setting, both inside and out. You're sure to pay as much attention to the views and the Philippe Starck interior as the food. Towering ceilings and copper-clad columns surround the Art-Deco tables. Even the view from the urinal is dizzying. The food is dainty, sometimes sublime, fusion (think lobster nachos).
✉ **The Peninsula, cnr**

Salisbury & Nathan Rds, Tsim Sha Tsui ☎ 2920 2888 (ext 3188) ◉ Tsim Sha Tsui ◷ 6pm-2am V

### Gaddi's (3, J5)    $$$$
*French*
Gaddi's maintains its reputation as the premier French restaurant in Hong Kong. It's boasted virtually the same menu (and some of the same staff) for 30 years. This is the sort of place where your grapes arrive peeled and sauces are routinely swirled with truffles or caviar. Romantic diners may enjoy one of the main courses served for two.
✉ **The Peninsula, cnr Salisbury & Nathan Rds** ☎ 2920 2888 (ext 3171) ◉ Tsim Sha Tsui ◷ noon-2.30pm, 7-11pm

### Gaylord (3, H4)    $$$
*Indian, Vegetarian*
Venerable Gaylord has been going strong since 1972. Dim lighting, booth seating and live Indian music usher you into a cosy world of spicy dining. You will hardly be able to tear yourself away from the

remains of chicken *tikka* and *pappadam* crumbs and return to the real world. There's a great lunch buffet.
✉ **23-25 Ashley Rd** ☎ 2376 1001 ◉ Tsim Sha Tsui ◷ noon-3pm, 6-11pm ♿ V

### Happy Garden Noodle & Congee Kitchen (3, G3)    $
*Chinese, Cantonese*
The Happy Garden cooks up some of Kowloon's best noodles and congee. It's a little more expensive than some of the backstreet joints but it's a heap more elegant and there's an English menu for those who are sick of pointing and pot luck.
✉ **76 Canton Rd** ☎ 2377 2604 ◉ Tsim Sha Tsui ◷ 7am-12.30am ♿ V

### Orphee (3, E6)    $$$
*French*
A small pocket of Paris in Tsim Sha Tsui. If you feel for a fill of *filet de boeuf* then Orphee will suffice.
✉ **18a Austin Ave** ☎ 2730 1128 ◉ Jordan ◷ noon-3pm, 7-11pm

## Kowloon City
Kai Tak Airport may have shut down but there's still culinary travelling to be done in Kowloon City. This is Hong Kong's Thai quarter and the area's restaurants are the place for a *tom yum* and green-curry fix. Expect a queue at the deservedly popular **Wong Chun Chun Thai Restaurant** (2, A3; ☎ 2716 6269; $$). The nearby **Golden Orchard Thai Restaurant** (2, A3; ☎ 2383 3076; $$) has secret spill-over rooms for when its restaurant fills up. Kowloon City, packed with herbalists, jewellers, tea merchants and bird shops is worth a pre- or post-dinner explore.

## Peking Restaurant
(3, D4) **$$**
*Chinese, Peking*
This place houses scurrying waiters and Peking duck fans merrily chomping away. If duck doesn't do it for you, try the Peking-style crab dishes and pastries.
✉ L1, 227 Nathan Rd
☎ 2730 1315
Ⓜ Jordan
🕑 11am-10.30pm

## Restaurant Osaka
(3, H4) **$$**
*Japanese*
A splash of class above the hustle of Ashley Rd, this atmospheric restaurant has pinafored waitresses and a menu that extends from sushi to steaks via hotpots. There are reasonably priced set lunches.
✉ 14 Ashley Rd
☎ 2376 3323 Ⓜ Tsim Sha Tsui 🕑 noon-3pm, 6-11pm Ⓥ

## Salisbury Dining Room
(3, J4) **$$$**
*International, Buffet*
Unlimited sushi and smoked salmon make the Salisbury buffets a pretty good bet. Book ahead if you want a table by the window and unimpeded harbour views. Guzzlers will be glad that the buffets include bottomless wine and draught beer.
✉ YMCA, 41 Salisbury Rd ☎ 2268 7000
Ⓜ Tsim Sha Tsui 🕑 Mon-Sat noon-2.30pm, daily 6.15-9.30pm ♿ Ⓥ

## Spring Deer
(3, H6) **$$$**
*Chinese*
Spring Deer, hidden up a smelly staircase in a nondescript building, serves some of the crispiest Peking duck in town. Although the atmosphere is none too flash, this place is extremely popular, so make sure to book well in advance.
✉ 42 Mody Rd ☎ 2366 4012 Ⓜ Tsim Sha Tsui 🕑 noon-2.30pm, 6-11pm

## Spring Moon
(3, J5) **$$$**
*Chinese, Cantonese*
Inside the grand Peninsula, Spring Moon is a most impressive restaurant. Complementing the high standards of the hotel, the Cantonese food is excellently prepared, and the ambience is stunning.
✉ The Peninsula, cnr Salisbury & Nathan Rds
☎ 2315 3160 Ⓜ Tsim Sha Tsui 🕑 11.30am-2.30pm, 6-10.30pm

## Sweet Dynasty
(3, G3) **$$**
*Chinese*
Sweet Dynasty has it all, from fine dim sum and tofu soups to congee big enough to swim in. It's a riot at lunch time but somehow retains a sense of style.
✉ 88 Canton Rd
☎ 2199 7799 Ⓜ Tsim Sha Tsui 🕑 10am-midnight ♿ Ⓥ

## Tokyo House
(3, E6) **$$**
*Japanese*
This cutely boothed eatery creates fresh and tasty set lunches for a fantastic price. And with 'lunch' extending to 6pm it's great for late hunger pangs. It also has Japanese beer and sake.
✉ 15 Austin Ave

---

---

## Whampoa Gourmet Place
**(2, B3)** $$

The face of one of Hong Kong's famous foodies, Choi Lam, festoons the walls of this gourmet complex in Hung Hom (east of Tsim Sha Tsui). He leers proudly over a dynamic mix of restaurants that include **Dow's Kitchen** (Cantonese – try the milky Shendu dishes), **Spicy Crab Restaurant** (guess its speciality) and **Noodles of Hong Kong** (ox is its forte, *all* parts thereof). If you can't find Whampoa Gourmet Place, just look for the massive boat-shaped building over the road.

✉ **L1, Whampoa Garden, 9 Shung King St, Hung Hom** ☎ **2128 7440** 🚌 **6, 8A** ◷ **11am-11pm** ⚓ V

---

☎ 2368 8984
🚇 Jordan ◷ noon-9pm ⚓

### A Touch of Spice
**(3, F6)** $$

*Indonesian, Vietnamese*
One of four trendy restaurant/bars stacked up at 10 Knutsford Terrace. This one does Indo-Viet curries, noodles and fry-ups. Most meals are good value, unless you go for the seafood – if you do want fish, you might rather try **Island Seafood** on the ground floor.

✉ 10 Knutsford Tce
☎ 2312 1118

🚇 Tsim Sha Tsui, Jordan ◷ noon-3pm, 6-11pm V

### Valentino
**(3, H6)** $$$

*Italian*
Romantic Italian classic with soft lights and nuzzling music. The seasonal menu has super soups (look out for a light tomato and zucchini broth in summer) and a good range of salads, pasta and meats.

✉ Ocean View Court, 27a Chatham Rd S
☎ 2721 6449 🚇 Tsim Sha Tsui ◷ noon-11pm V

### Wan Loong Court
**(3, J4)** $$$$

*Chinese, Cantonese*
Wonderful Cantonese food with deft modern touches: the dim sum here takes some beating. Standout dumplings include steamed beef with tangerine peel, and the house dessert is tai chi cake, a chestnut paste and poppy seed pastry. There's an English menu and service is great.

✉ Kowloon Hotel, 19-21 Nathan Rd ☎ 2734 3722 🚇 Tsim Sha Tsui ◷ Mon-Fri 11am-3pm, 6-11.30pm, Sat-Sun 11am-11.30pm V

## TSIM SHA TSUI EAST

### Fruit Stop (3, F6) $

*Chinese*
Student hang-out with a jazz soundtrack and a battalion of shiny young folk on deck. The decor is plastic but the food is healthy. Crunch on cornflakes, fresh fruit and vegetable juices and a wacky selection of sandwiches – how's banana and cinnamon? Not weird enough? Try strawberry yoghurt on toast. There are noodles too

if you want to keep it Asian. There's also a branch in Harbour City, Tsim Sha Tsui (3, H3).

✉ Toyo Mall, 94 Granville Rd ☎ 2973 6873 🚇 Tsim Sha Tsui ◷ Mon-Sat 7.30am-10.30pm, Sun noon-10.30pm ⚓ V

### Sabatini (3, G7) $$$

*Italian*
Classy Sabatini is a direct copy of its namesake in

Rome, with designs painted on the walls and ceilings, and a polished tile floor. Even classic Italian dishes, such as fettuccine carbonara, come across as light in the best sense, leaving room to sample the exquisite desserts. The wine list is also excellent.

✉ Royal Garden Hotel, 69 Mody Rd ☎ 2733 2000 🚇 Tsim Sha Tsui ◷ noon-2.30pm, 6-11pm

# VICTORIA PEAK

### Cafe Deco (4, K2) $$$
*International*

The philosophy seems to be that views, live jazz and buzzy ambience are enough to keep the punters happy. And if you stick to cocktails and simple fresh food (the oyster bar, the sushi) you won't go too wrong. But the more artistry the food attempts, the more it falls down.

✉ Peak Galleria, 118 Peak Rd ☎ 2849 5111 🚌 15 (from Exchange Sq), minibus 1 (from Star Ferry) ⊙ Sun-Thurs 10am-midnight, Fri-Sat 10am-1am (kitchen closes 11.30pm) **V**

### Peak Lookout
(4, K2) $$$
*International*

East meets West at the Peak. The food is always delicious, and includes Chinese, Indian, Thai and some Western dishes (the Indian food is usually the best bet). What really makes this place is the

*The view from the Peak makes for memorable dining*

amazing setting: a vaulted ceiling, elegant decor and one of Hong Kong's finest bars. There's a large outdoor terrace that is very romantic on a warm evening.

✉ 121 Peak Rd ☎ 2532 6227 🚌 15 (from Exchange Sq), minibus 1 (from Star Ferry) ⊙ 10.30am-midnight (kitchen closes 10.45pm) **V**

### Restaurant Marché
(4, K2) $$
*International*

Wander over and order from hawker market-style kitchenettes offering roasts, curries, grills, pasta, sushi and more. Buffet specials are available at lunch and from around 10pm. There are several different eating areas, most of them with spectacular views from the Peak Tower. This is a great place to bring kids: there's a play area and lots of child-friendly food.

✉ L6-7, Peak Tower, 128 Peak Rd (enter from L4) ☎ 2849 2000 🚌 15 (from Exchange Sq), minibus 1 (from Star Ferry) ⊙ 10.30am-midnight (kitchen closes 10.45pm) ♿ **V**

## Tasty Views

If you're a sucker for a view, you're going to love Hong Kong. The best ground-level views are looking back across the harbour from Tsim Sha Tsui, most notably from **Yu** (3, K5; ☎ 2721 1211; $$$$), the topnotch seafood restaurant in the waterfront Inter-Continental.

On the island side, the best views are from on high. **R66** (4, H12; ☎ 2862 6166; $$$), 62nd fl, Hopewell Centre, 183 Queen's Rd E, Wan Chai, obeys the unwritten code of revolving restaurants by playing cheesy music, serving average buffets and meals with a surf 'n' turf angle. It's best to roll up for an afternoon coffee or a fruity cocktail and go for a spin. To go up in the outfacing bubble lifts, change at the 17th floor (lifts 27 and 28 in the alcove opposite lift 6).

If you want a bit more class, try **Scenario** (4, D4; ☎ 2186 6868; $$$), 42nd fl, The Center, 99 Queen's Rd Central, Central. The food is classic Italian but you can sit in the lounge for a drink and a snack.

Other good-for-gawping restaurants are those at **Victoria Peak** (p. 84), **Spring Moon** (p. 82), **Felix** (p. 81) and **Port Cafe** (p. 86).

# WAN CHAI

## Amaroni's Little Italy
**(4, H12)** $$$
*American Italian*
The first rule of American-Italian cuisine is 'make it big'. And Amaroni's doesn't disappoint with serves of pasta, seafood and steak so large that they make the floor staff strain. Kids get a free feed during the week.
✉ **Shop 3-4, Wu Chung House, 213 Queen's Rd E** ☎ 2891 8555
🚇 Wan Chai ◷ Mon-Fri 11am-midnight, Sat-Sun 10am-midnight ♿

## American Restaurant
**(4, G11)** $$
*Chinese*
Don't be put off by the name or by the grimy appearance. The friendly American has been serving excellent Peking cuisine for over 50 years. Most of its customers are regulars. As you'd hope, the Peking duck and the beggar's chicken (order in advance) are very good.
✉ **Goldenstar Bldg, 20 Lockhart Rd** ☎ 2527 1000 🚇 Wan Chai ◷ 11am-11.30pm ♿

## Carrianna Chiu Chow Restaurant
**(4, F14)** $$$
*Chinese, Chiu Chow*
For Chiu Chow food, the Carrianna rates right up there. Try the cold dishes (goose slices and cold crab), pork with tofu, or chicken with *chin jew* sauce. The place is usually crowded, but there are plenty of tables.
✉ **AXA Centre, 151 Gloucester Rd (enter from Tonnochy Rd)** ☎ 2511 1282
🚇 Wan Chai ◷ 11am-midnight ♿

## Dynasty
**(4, E12)** $$$
*Chinese, Cantonese*
Stylish Cantonese restaurant that does a much-lauded daily dim sum. This is a good choice for business lunches: the atmosphere is more hum and hush than the normal dim sum clatter. If you're ordering from the menu, try the shredded beef with water chestnuts and tangerine peel.
✉ **Renaissance Harbour View Hotel, 1 Harbour Rd** ☎ 2802 8888 (ext 6971)
🚇 Wan Chai ◷ noon-2.30pm, 6.30-10.30pm

## Fook Lam Moon
**(4, G11)** $$$$
*Chinese*
Long known as one of Hong Kong's top Cantonese restaurants, Fook Lam Moon makes sure you're taken care of from the minute you walk in the door. Seafood is the speciality: try the pan-fried lobster balls. Also at Luna Court, 53-59 Kimberley Rd, Tsim Sha Tsui (3, F6).
✉ **35-45 Johnston Rd** ☎ 2866 0663 🚇 Wan Chai ◷ 11.30am-3pm, 6-11pm ♿

## New Taste Restaurant
**(4, G12)** $$
*Indian, Nepalese*
The clutter and clang of this tile-rich restaurant is all Hong Kong, but the vindaloos and *momos* are undoubtedly subcontinental. A friendly no fuss place with a wide selection of curries, naan and vegetable dishes.
✉ **100-102 Jaffe Rd** ☎ 2866 2869 🚇 Wan Chai ◷ Mon-Fri 6-11pm, Sat-Sun 11am-11pm ♿ **V**

## Business with a Bite
A lot of expense-account wining and dining occurs at hotel restaurants: in Tsim Sha Tsui consider the Hyatt's **Chinese Restaurant** (p. 81), and **Avenue** (3, H5; ☎ 2315 1118; $$$$) in the Holiday Inn Golden Mile, 50 Nathan Rd. On Hong Kong Island, the Renaissance Harbour View's **Dynasty** (p. 85) is right by the Convention & Exhibition Centre while **Vong** (p. 73) in the Mandarin Oriental is as central as it gets.

Good lunch spots where you can talk without shouting include **The Square** (p. 73) and **Port Cafe** (p. 86). **Va Bene** (p. 74) and **Boca** (p. 75) are great places to take the team when you've sealed the deal.

## Open Kitchen
**(4, F11)** $$
*International*
When your cafeteria serves up delicious Indian, Malay and Italian meals, and you have a harbour view on which to marvel while you munch, you know you're on the right track. Open Kitchen is a good, arty option for meals, snacks or drinks at the bar. Bring your ticket stub from the cinema downstairs to get a free drink with your meal.
✉ **Hong Kong Arts Centre, 2 Harbour Rd** ☎ 2827 2923 🚇 Wan Chai ◷ 11am-11pm ♿ **V**

**Port Cafe (4, D12) $$$**
*International*
The Port is sophisticated yet relaxed, and serves fine Italian and Asian cuisine. A refined Asian-style high tea is served weekdays. You're jutting out into the harbour so the views are stunning. Note it's not open for dinner.
✉ **Convention & Exhibition Centre, 1 Expo Dr** ☎ **2582 7731** Ⓜ **Wan Chai** ⏱ **Mon-Sun 11am-6pm (high tea: Mon-Fri 3-6pm)** Ⓥ

**Steam and Stew Inn (4, H11) $$**
*Chinese*
The Inn serves 'home-style' Cantonese food – steamed, stewed or boiled. Try the steamed mushroom stuffed with minced pork and crab-meat sauce. It's popular, so consider booking ahead.
✉ **Hing Wong Court, 21-23 Tai Wong St E** ☎ **2529 3913** Ⓜ **Wan Chai** ⏱ **11.30am-2.30pm, 5.30-11.30pm**

**Super Star Seafood Restaurant (4, F12) $$**
*Chinese, Cantonese*
Plastic pictures on the menu and a pink satin explosion on the back wall. Lucky the kitchen comes through as a super star, serving up delectable dim sum (grilled eel, stone fish roll, chicken in wine marinade). The army of staff are happy to help you where the food photos fail.
✉ **1st fl, Shui On Centre, 8 Harbour Rd** ☎ **2802 8182** Ⓜ **Wan Chai** ⏱ **11am-11pm** ♿

**369 Shanghai Restaurant (4, F12) $$**
*Chinese, Shanghainese*
Low-key Shanghai food that's nothing like five-star but does the dumpling job. It's family-run and there are some good comfy booths in the window. It's open late too, so you can come here after a draining dance.
✉ **30-32 O'Brien Rd** ☎ **2527 2343** Ⓜ **Wan Chai** ⏱ **noon-4am** ♿

# YAU MA TEI

**Bali Restaurant (3, C5) $$**
*Indonesian*
The food is pretty good and the service is friendly but the best thing about Bali Restaurant is its superb tackiness: a permanent 'happy birthday' sign, vinyl booths separated by fake brick walls and a 'resort'-style bar. Try the yellow rice special dish (pictured on the Chinese menu) and the pork satays.
✉ **10 Nanking St (off Nathan Rd)** ☎ **2780 2902** Ⓜ **Jordan** ⏱ **noon-11pm** ♿

**Hing Kee (3, A4) $**
*Chinese*
You won't find Hing Kee if you're looking for its name in lights so keep an eye out for earthen pots filled with rice cooking out on the streets. This is just one choice in a glut of good-value night-time dining choices at the top end of Temple St Night Market (p. 26).
✉ **19 Temple St (enter from Hi Lung Lane)** ☎ **2384 3647** Ⓜ **Yau Ma Tei** ⏱ **5.30pm-midnight** ♿

**Joyful Vegetarian (2, B2) $$**
*Vegetarian*
This popular restaurant serves up great all-vegetarian meals. The vegetable country-style hotpot is made with a ravishing range of fungi. There's a snack stall out the front if you need a bite on the fly.
✉ **530 Nathan Rd (nth of Waterloo Rd; see p. 47)** ☎ **2780 2230** Ⓜ **Yau Ma Tei** ⏱ **11am-11pm** ♿ Ⓥ

**Miu Gute Cheong Vegetarian Restaurant (3, C4) $**
*Chinese, Vegetarian*
Cheap, cheerful and family-oriented vegetarian restaurant. The tofu is fresh and firm, the vegetables are the pick of the market and the tea flows freely.
✉ **31 Ning Po St** ☎ **2771 6217** Ⓜ **Yau Ma Tei** ⏱ **11am-11pm** ♿ Ⓥ

## Street-side Sustenance
Mong Kok and Yau Ma Tei are the best areas for street food; a night-time stroll through both the Ladies' Market (cnr Tung Choi & Dundas Sts) and Temple St Night Market (at Wing Sing Lane intersection) will be punctuated with alluring smells from woks and braziers. It's a point-and-guess affair but the cooks are used to inquisitive customers, so don't slink off unsatisfied. Look for fried snacks, dim sum (look for piles of steaming baskets) and wok-fried noodles.

# entertainment

When you want to be wowed, Hong Kong is a capable entertainer. Most weeks, half a dozen local arts companies perform anything from Cantonese opera to an English-language version of a Chekhov play. Locally cultivated drama and dance is among the best in Asia, and the schedule of foreign performances is also often impressive – recent imports have included the Pet Shop Boys and the Budapest Concert Orchestra. Luckily, the government subsidises the cost of international acts, so ticket prices can be very reasonable: around $50 for a seat up the back for a local performance and up to $300 for a top-class international act.

This isn't to say that Hong Kong is a cultural honey pot. Many government initiatives appear more motivated by the idea that Hong Kong *should* be an arty town, than by a heartfelt commitment to artistic endeavour. Art generally plays second fiddle to commerce, sometimes with a comic outcome – when residents complained about noise spillage from stadium concerts, suggested solutions included turning off the stage speakers and issuing concert-goers with headphones.

## Top Spots

The biggest bar crawl is definitely **Lan Kwai Fong**, a narrow L-shaped alley in Central lined with nightspots. The clientele is upwardly mobile: ruddy expats mix with local business types and trendies. Nearby **Soho** has more of a restaurant scene and a number of bars have opened along the escalator route and its cross streets. The newest hang-out is **Boho** (BelOw HOllywood Rd), where some slick gay/straight bars and clubs have cropped up.

**Wan Chai** is sleaze territory, with awful hostess bars along Lockhart Rd and lots of zippy club action and late-night covers-band venues. It's the part of town that kicks on latest – handy if it's dawn and you still want to dance.

**Kowloon** has more of a local Chinese scene. There are three basic clusters of bars in Tsim Sha Tsui: along Ashley Rd; areas west of Chatham Rd (Austin Ave, Prat Ave); and up by Knutsford Terrace. Tsim Sha Tsui East is swanky hostess-bar territory.

## Information

The *South China Morning Post* has daily arts and entertainment listings and a Sunday liftout – most content is available online ( **e** www.totally hk.com). Free local magazines, *HK* and *bc* are up on club nights, drinks deals and happy hours, art exhibitions and performances. The HKTB has several free information publications, including the monthly *Official Hong Kong Guide* and the weekly *What's On*. The Hong Kong Arts Centre publishes *Artslink* monthly, with listings of exhibitions and art-house film screenings. *Gaystation* is a monthly gay-centric listings publication.

## Bookings

Bookings for most cultural events can be made through URBTIX ( ☎ 2734 9009; **e** www.urbtix.gov.hk; 10am-8pm). Another concert and show booker is Cityline ( ☎ 2317 6666; **e** www.cityline.com.hk).

## SPECIAL EVENTS

**late January/early February** *Chinese New Year* – fireworks, flower fairs
*Yuen Siu (Lantern Festival)* – following New Year traditional lanterns are displayed throughout the city and paraded through the streets
*Fringe Festival* – eclectic performances sponsored by the Fringe Club

**February** *Hong Kong Arts Festival* – month-long series of performing arts events
*Golf Open* – at the Royal Hong Kong Golf Club
*International Marathon* – held in Sha Tin

**March** *Food Festival* – seasonal food fair with tastings and excursions

**late March/early April** *Hong Kong Rugby Sevens* – this famous three-day carnival is the city's biggest sporting event
*Hong Kong International Film Festival* – a cinematic showcase from Hong Kong and the rest of the world

**April/May** *Tin Hau Festival* – celebrations on the water in honour of the patroness of fishing people

**May** *Cheung Chau Bun Festival* – three-day Taoist munch and march

**June** *Dragon Boat Festival* – boat races and fireworks

**mid-July** *International Arts Carnival* – focuses on the Cultural Centre with performances around town
*Hong Kong Fashion Week* – parades and events at the Convention & Exhibition Centre and at shopping centres around town
*Food Expo* – festival of the munch at the Convention & Exhibition Centre

**mid-September** *Mid-Autumn Festival* – romantic moon-watching celebration

**late September/early October** *International Cricket Series* – two-day event

**October** *Festival of Asian Arts* – one of Asia's major cultural events; biennial
*Hong Kong Youth Arts Festival* – young talent perform at various venues
*Chung Yeung Festival* – mountain picnics and family visits to graves

**November** *Hong Kong Folk Festival* – international and local performers

**December** *Euro-Christmas* – turkey basting and tree decorating
*International Cantonese Opera Festival* – local and foreign troupes

*Prayers for a new year*

# CLASSICAL ARTS & COMEDY

### City Hall (4, E7)

Hosts classical recitals, Chinese music concerts and lots of dance. City Contemporary Dance Company is an exciting local outfit that performs here. Recent productions combined dance, striptease and video, and choreographers shared the billing with fashion designers.

✉ **Concert Hall, City Hall, 7 Edinburgh Pl, Central** ☎ 2921 2840; bookings: 2734 9009 Ⓜ Central Ⓢ $100-200

### Fringe Theatres

(6, E5) The two theatres here host eclectic local and international performances in both Cantonese and English. There's usually something worth seeing.

✉ **2 Lower Albert Rd, Lan Kwai Fong** ☎ 2521 7251 Ⓜ Central Ⓢ $50-200

### Hong Kong Academy for Performing Arts

(4, F11) Stages local and overseas performances of dance, drama and music. The building was designed by local architect Simon Kwan.

✉ **1 Gloucester Rd, Wan Chai** ☎ info: 2584 8500; box office: 2584 8514 Ⓜ Wan Chai 🚌 10A, 20, 21

### Hong Kong Arts Centre (4, F11)

This independent showcase for contemporary arts in all media emphasises home-grown talent. The theatre here hosts drama (often in English) by local companies such as the Hong Kong Players. The centre

---

### Opera Outdoors

**Cantonese opera** is performed nightly at the corner of Temple St and Jordan Rd N (at the top of the night market) between 7pm and 11pm. The second Sunday of each month (2.30pm to 5.30pm) sees **Harbourfront Fest** in the forecourt of the Hong Kong Cultural Centre. Performers range from acrobats to choirs. The **International Cantonese Opera Festival** takes place in December.

---

publishes a monthly listings magazine, *Insight*. See also Pao Galleries (p. 39) and Lim Por Yen Theatre (p. 90).

✉ **2 Harbour Rd, Wan Chai** ☎ 2582 0200 Ⓜ Wan Chai 🚌 10A, 20, 21 Ⓢ $50-200

### Hong Kong Cultural Centre (3, K4)

With three large theatres, this is Hong Kong's premier performance venue, with regular Chinese music and opera performances. It's also home to the Hong Kong Repertory Theatre, Hong Kong Philharmonic Orchestra, and major touring companies usually play here.

✉ **cnr Salisbury & Canton Rds, Tsim Sha Tsui** ☎ 2734 2009 Ⓜ Tsim Sha Tsui Ⓢ $100-300

### Sunbeam Theatre

(2, C3) Cantonese opera can be seen here throughout the year. Performances generally run for about a week, and are usually held in the evening. The theatre is right above North Point MTR, on the northern side of King's Rd, near the intersection with Shu Kuk St – look for the garish posters.

✉ **Kiu Fai Bldg, 423 King's Rd, North Point** ☎ 2563 2959 Ⓜ North Point Ⓢ $50-300 ♿

### Viceroy (4, F14)

The Viceroy is the scene of one-off live bands, dance parties, salsa nights and the Punchline Comedy Club.

✉ **2nd fl, Sun Hung Kai Centre, 30 Harbour Rd, Wan Chai** ☎ 2827 7777 Ⓜ Wan Chai ⏲ noon-3pm, 6-11pm Ⓢ shows: $200-300

*Fringe Theatre, Central*

# CINEMAS

Most cinemas screen five sessions daily: 12.30pm, 2.30pm, 5.30pm, 7.30pm and 9.30pm with extra 4pm and 11.30pm screenings on weekends. Almost all Hong Kong films have English subtitles. Admission is usually $50 (half-price on Tuesday).

**Broadway Cinematheque** (3, A3)
An unlikely place for an alternative cinema but it's worth checking out for new art-house releases and rerun screenings. There's a café next door that serves good coffee and decent pre-flick food.
✉ 3 Public Sq St, Yau Ma Tei ☎ 2388 0002
🚇 Yau Ma Tei ♿

**Cine-Art House**
(4, F14) This alternative cinema specialises in English-language flicks.
✉ Sun Hung Kai Centre, 30 Harbour Rd, Wan Chai ☎ 2827 4820 🚇 Wan Chai ♿

**Hong Kong Film Archive** (2, C4)
The place to find out what lies behind Hong Kong's hard-boiled film industry. The archive houses 3800 films, runs a rich calendar of screenings (local and foreign) and exhibits natty posters and other fine film paraphernalia. You may even see Bruce Lee with his shirt on.
✉ 50 Lei King Rd, Sai Wan Ho ☎ 2739 2139
🚇 Sai Wan Ho
🕐 exhibition space & library: 10am-8pm (phone for screenings)

**JP Cinema** (5, E3)
Thanks to JP's there's no problem finding mainstream flicks in Causeway Bay. Be prepared for huge crowds

*Nothing art house about the Silvercord*

on weekends.
✉ JP Plaza, 22-36 Paterson St (cnr Great George St), Causeway Bay ☎ 2881 5005
🚇 Causeway Bay ♿

**Lim Por Yen Theatre**
(4, F11) The Lim Por Yen is the place for classics, revivals, alternative screenings and travelling film festivals. The annual European Film Festival is usually held here in November.
✉ Hong Kong Arts Centre, 2 Harbour Rd, Wan Chai ☎ information: 2582 0232; reservations: 2582 0200
🚇 Wan Chai ♿

**Queen's Theatre**
(4, E5) Queen's is one of the only movie houses in Central geared towards English-language films. It's a great old barn of a place and a very atmospheric spot to catch a film.
✉ Luk Hoi Tung Bldg, 31 Queen's Rd (rear entrance), Central

☎ 2522 7036
🚇 Central 🅿 yes ♿

**Silvercord Cinema**
(3, G3) The easy-to-find Silvercord is just along from the Star Ferry terminal. Its two theatres screen the latest Hollywood releases. Just up the road is the **Ocean Theatre**
(☎ 2377 2100), Harbour City, 3 Canton Rd.
✉ 30 Canton Rd, Tsim Sha Tsui ☎ 2388 3188
🚇 Tsim Sha Tsui ♿

**UA Queensway**
(4, G9) It's blessedly easy to sink your seat into the comfort offered by Hong Kong's plushest cinema. Its great sound system ensures you won't miss a whisper. There's also a big UA complex in Times Square (5, G2; ☎ 2506 2822) right above the MTR.
✉ Pacific Place, 88 Queensway, Admiralty ☎ 2869 0322
🚇 Admiralty 🅿 yes ♿

# GAY & LESBIAN HONG KONG

The last few years have seen the Hong Kong gay scene strengthen. Bars and clubs have popped up around Soho as well as over in Tsim Sha Tsui. Grab a copy of *Gaystation* or visit [e] www.gaystation.com.hk for updated nightlife, shopping and sauna-scene info.

## Club 64 (6, D4)

A gay bar but by no means preference specific. This funky hang-out is named after the Tiananmen Square massacre (64 stands for the date of the massacre: 4th of the 6th month) and is still one of the best bars for those who want simple, unfussy fun.
✉ **Winner Bldg, 12 Wing Wah Lane, Lan Kwai Fong** ☎ **2523 2801** Ⓜ Central
🕐 Sun-Thurs 3pm-1am, Fri-Sat 3pm-3am

## Home (6, C3)

A meet 'n' greet for the beautiful people early, turning into a bump 'n' grind later in the evening. This is one of the only places in Hong Kong that hosts 'girls who like girls' nights. Has karaoke on Monday evening.
✉ **2nd fl, 23 Hollywood Rd, Central** ☎ **2545 0023** Ⓜ Central 🕐 Mon-Fri 7pm-3am, Sat 10pm-6am

## Propaganda (6, C4)

As its ads are proud to proclaim, this is Hong Kong's premier gay meat market. It's free from Monday to Wednesday, but charges creep up towards the weekend. Inside, there's a long undulating bar and plenty of mirrors so you can talent-spot.
✉ **1 Hollywood Rd (enter from Ezra's Lane, off Cochrane St), Boho** ☎ **2868 1316** Ⓜ Central 🕐 Mon-Thurs 9pm-2.30am, Fri-Sat 9pm-4am Ⓢ $90-160 Fri-Sat

## Rice Bar (4, C3)

Rice is a small, vibey gay bar with a lounge area that sees a bit of dancing as it gets later. On-site tarot card and palm readers can help you out with life's important questions. If the answer is eating, there's cute food to be had on site.
✉ **33 Jervois St (cnr Mercer St), Sheung Wan** ☎ **2851 4800** Ⓜ Sheung Wan 🚻 yes 🕐 6.30pm-2am

## Wally Matt Lounge (3, F6)

Canton pop karaoke and *It's raining men* remixes ring through this boy-zone. It's dark and industrial but there are plenty of seats if you decide to retreat with a drink and watch the action.
✉ **3a Granville Circuit, Tsim Sha Tsui** ☎ **2367 6874** Ⓜ Tsim Sha Tsui 🕐 8pm-late

## Works (6, E5)

This dark club is the midway point on a long night out for most and sees some heavy cruising.
✉ **L1, 30-32 Wyndham St, Central** ☎ **2868 6102** 🕐 Tues-Sun 7pm-2am Ⓢ $60 including drink

*Bright lights, shapes, shadows and silhouettes*

# CLUBS & KARAOKE

The club scene is hot and vibed up. Cover charges ($50-200) sometimes include a drink or two and entrance can be free on particular theme nights. Hong Kong's raves are advertised in *HK*, *bc* and online at [e] hkclubber.com or [e] www.hkrave.com.

### Bahama Mama's Caribbean Bar (3, F5)

Bahama Mama's theme is tropical isle, complete with palm trees and surfboards. It's a friendly spot and stands apart from most of the other late-night watering holes. On Friday and Saturday nights there's a DJ spinning and folks out on the bonsai-sized dance floor.
✉ 4-5 Knutsford Tce, Tsim Sha Tsui ☎ 2368 2121 ⊕ Tsim Sha Tsui, Jordan ⊙ Sun-Thurs 5pm-3am, Fri-Sat 5pm-4am

### Big Apple (4, F12)

The Big Apple is frequently nominated as one of Hong Kong's raunchiest nightspots. It's busiest on Sunday nights when Indonesians on their day off, go off. Go and have a look at the great neon sign even if you're not up for a dance.
✉ 20 Luard Rd, Wan Chai ☎ 2529 3461 ⊕ Wan Chai ⊙ Mon-Thurs 4pm-4am, Fri-Sun 2pm-4am

### Club de Millennium (3, G5)

If your wallet is fat this club will most likely let you partake of its high-class giggly sleaze where hostesses are rented by the minute and drinks are expensive. There are lavish harem-style lounges done up as Gucci and Versace showrooms.
✉ 10-11th fl, BCC Bldg, 25-31 Carnarvon Rd (enter from Hanoi Rd), Tsim Sha Tsui ☎ 2723 5088 ⊕ Tsim Sha Tsui ⊙ 8.30pm-4am ⑤ $150 (for starters)

### Club ing (4, E12)

Newly decked-out club with chatting lounges, a long bar, karaoke and disco. It's popular with a young Cantonese crowd. Dress smartly. There's free entry and drinks for fashionable ladies on Thursday night.
✉ L4, Renaissance Harbour View Hotel, 1 Harbour Rd, Wan Chai ☎ 2836 3690 ⊕ Wan Chai ⊙ 8pm-late ⑤ $100+

### Club 97 (6, D5)

A schmoozery that uses a selectively enforced 'members only' policy to turn away the badly dressed. There's a sceney gay happy hour on Friday night, with free entry and half-price drinks. **Post 97**, the restaurant next door, has the same management.
✉ Cosmos Bldg, 9-11 Lan Kwai Fong, Lan Kwai Fong ☎ 2586 1103 ⊕ Central ⊙ Mon-Fri 5pm-5am, Sat 10pm-5am, Sun 10pm-4am

### Drop (6, C3)

Deluxe lounge action, fat tunes and potent fresh lychee cocktails are what keeps Drop strong. It's like walking into *Wallpaper* magazine, but the vibe here is unpretentiously inclusive. Flexible members-only policy after 11pm on Friday and Saturday is enforced to keep the dance floor capacity at manageable sardine level.
✉ Basement, On Lok Mansion, 39-43 Hollywood Rd, Central ☎ 2543 8856 [e] www.drophk.com ⊕ Central ⊙ 7pm-late

### Energy Karaoke (3, G5)

New-fangled karaoke club with private booths: come with friends to choose from hundreds of songs in Chinese, Korean, Japanese and English and belt them out in your own padded cell. You can hear the

*Dress smartly for Club ing at the Renaissance*

warbling of wannabe pop-stars through the corridors.
✉ **8 Humphreys Ave (cnr Cameron St), Tsim Sha Tsui** ☎ **2366 3388** Ⓜ **Tsim Sha Tsui** ⏰ **noon-6am** ⓢ **free for first 3hrs if you order drinks** ♿

### JB's (4, F12)
Newly renovated JB's (Joe Banana's) has dropped its long-standing wet T-shirt aesthetic and gone for more of a bamboo-bar feel. Unaccompanied females should expect a good sampler of bad pick-up lines.
✉ **Shiu Lam Bldg, 23 Luard Rd (cnr Jaffe Rd), Wan Chai** ☎ **2529 1811** Ⓜ **Wan Chai** ⏰ **Mon-Thurs 11am-5am, Fri-Sat 11am-6am, Sun 3pm-5am** ⓢ **$100 Fri & Sat after 10.30pm**

### JJ's (4, E12)
Not as suity as you might think – this is disco for Hong Kong's divine dahlings with DJs spinning funky house from 10pm nightly except Sunday. Live bands are now being squeezed into the schedule. Dress up.
✉ **Grand Hyatt, 1 Harbour Rd, Wan Chai** ☎ **2588 1234 (ext 7323)** Ⓜ **Wan Chai** ⏰ **Mon-Thurs 6pm-2am, Fri 6pm-3am, Sat 7pm-4am** ⓢ **$100-200**

### Liquid (6, B2)
This post-work suit hang-out makes an easy transition to sceney DJ zone. Sunday sees singers and musicians added to the mix.
✉ **1-5 Elgin St, Central** ☎ **2517 3310** ⏰ **6pm-late** ⓢ **varies**

### Neptune Disco II
**(4, F12)** Neptune II is a fun club with a mostly Filipino crowd and a rockin' covers band. If everything's closing and you can't bear to stop dancing, this is definitely the place to come.
✉ **98-108 Jaffe Rd, Wan Chai** ☎ **2865 2238** Ⓜ **Wan Chai** ⏰ **Mon-Thurs 4pm-5am, Fri-Sun 2pm-5am** ⓢ **$50-150**

### New Tonnochy Nightclub (4, F14)
Wan Chai's hostess bars have just reached a new zenith (or nadir) of uber-opulence. The decor here is a bizarre mishmash of Hapsburg meets Ming dynasty and drinks and inane chitchat with topless staff comes at an absurd price. You have been warned.
✉ **1-5 Tonnochy Rd, Wan Chai** ☎ **2511 1383** Ⓜ **Wan Chai** ⏰ **6pm-3am** ⓢ **$150+**

### One-Fifth (4, G9)
This is the club that matches your Prada outfit: an undulating, polished-floorboard entrance brings you to a broad bar backed by a two-storey drinks selection. Clubs located this far from the pack have to lure punters somehow.
✉ **Starcrest, 9 Star St, Wan Chai** ☎ **2520 2515** Ⓜ **Admiralty, Wan Chai** ⏰ **7pm-late**

### PMM (2, D3)
Wednesday night is 'model's night' at PMM, when the city's svelte drape on chairs and sip Moet. It's a highly charged shmoozery, with more interest in mwah-mwahing around the room than the R&B/rap DJ. Most people know this place as Pink Mao Mao, a moniker the club can't shake.
✉ **3rd fl, Emperor Happy Valley Hotel, 1 Wang Tak St, Happy Valley** ☎ **2961 3350** ⏰ **9pm-3am**

## Going Solo
Fun for one is not impossible. Going alone is the best way to meet locals and cover more ground without having to address a delegation. Soho in Central and Austin Ave in Tsim Sha Tsui are two areas thick with relaxed bars that you can peruse and stay for a drink. **Gecko** (p. 95), **Club Feather Boa** (p. 95) and **Chemical Suzy** (p. 95) are relaxed but happening places. Lan Kwai Fong is a more highly charged pick-up zone. Wan Chai is girly bar land and touters will assume you're on the prowl.

Dinner alone in a swanky restaurant may make you feel scroogish – just you and an army of attentive waiters – but in a business-trip capital like Hong Kong, solo dining is prevalent. Perhaps go for food with a view so you're not stuck watching other diners (p. 84). Most lunch time, dim sum and no-frills noodle restaurants have tables set aside for those going alone, so you can dine together solitarily.

# LIVE MUSIC

There is virtually no local original-music scene in Hong Kong. The Fringe Club is just about the only place an indie band could play, but it's no CBGBs. Live music usually means Filipino pop bands playing MOR covers in hotel lounges. Check the Information section (p. 87) for listings.

### Blue Door (6, B3)
A relaxed jazz venue with free music and good food from the upstairs Sichuanese restaurant.
✉ L5, 37 Cochrane St, Central (enter from Gage St) ☎ 2858 6555 🚇 Central ⏱ live music from 10.30pm

### Blue Note (3, H7)
You know the owners are trying hard when they call their club after the most famous jazz spot in the world. There's mostly imported talent on a rotating residency basis every night except Sunday.
✉ Kowloon Shangri-La Hotel, 64 Mody Rd, Tsim Sha Tsui East ☎ 2721 2111 🚇 Tsim Sha Tsui ⏱ 5pm-1am

### Chasers (3, F5)
A friendly, sorta classy pub with a live Filipino covers band nightly from 9.30pm. Before the band cranks up, there's a jukebox to party with. It serves a bar menu until midnight and snacks until 4am. There's dancing

most nights; the weekend sees a major sweat-fest.
✉ 2-3 Knutsford Tce, Tsim Sha Tsui ☎ 2367 9487 🚇 Tsim Sha Tsui, Jordan ⏱ Mon-Fri 4pm-5am, Sat-Sun noon-5am

### Dusk till Dawn
(4, G12) Live music from 9.30pm with an emphasis on beats and vibes so irresistible that you'll get your booty shaking. The dance floor can be packed but the atmosphere is usually more friendly than sleazy. Food sticks to easy fillers like meat pies and burgers.
✉ 76-84 Jaffe Rd, Wan Chai ☎ 2528 4689 🚇 Wan Chai ⏱ Mon-Sat noon-5am, Sun 3pm-5am 💲 $100+

### Fringe Club (6, E5)
The Fringe, a friendly venue on the border of the Lan Kwai Fong quadrant, has original music in the gallery/bar Friday and Saturday nights with jazz, rock and world music getting the most airplay. In summer, there's a 'secret'

bar on the roof.
✉ 2 Lower Albert Rd, Lan Kwai Fong ☎ 2521 7251 🚇 Central ⏱ shows Thurs, Fri & Sat from 10.30pm

### Music Room (6, D5)
Live music every night, but it could be rock, pop, Cuban, congo disco, R&B or funk. No cover charge makes this central venue nothing of a gamble.
✉ 2nd fl, California Entertainment Bldg, 34 D'Aguilar St, Lan Kwai Fong ☎ 2845 8477 🚇 Central ⏱ 5.30pm-1am

### The Wanch (4, F11)
The Wanch has live music seven nights a week from 9pm, mostly rock and folk, with the occasional solo guitarist thrown in. Jam night is Monday. If you're not there for the music it's a dubious scene – the Wanch is basically a pick-up joint.
✉ 54 Jaffe Rd, Wan Chai ☎ 2861 1621 🚇 Wan Chai ⏱ 11am-4am

## Cantopop
Hong Kong's popular music is generically known as Cantopop, a saccharine arrangement of romantic melodies and lyrics. Rarely radical, the songs invariably deal with teen issues such as unrequited puppy love, loneliness and high emotion. The music is polished and compulsively singable (hence the explosion of karaoke parlours). Big names in the music industry are thespian/crooner Andy Lau, Candy Lo and Twins.

# BARS & PUBS

Much of Hong Kong's nightlife takes place in top-end hotels where alluring happy hours, skilled bar staff and some of the best views in town attract visitors and locals. There's also many a stylish bar where the clothes are straight out of the bag, the sounds are smooth, the drinks are electric and the buzz is hardcore gossip. Unsurprisingly, British-style pubs are also plentiful – especially in tourist areas. Often British or Australian owned, they have authentic decor, meat pies, darts and sport on the TV.

## Style Bars

**Alibi** (6, D4)
This sleek Soho bar has a few tricks up its staircase, including a late-night brassiere and the occasional all-organic buffet. Down at the bar it's all wine, cocktails and a DJ to pep up the punters.
✉ **73 Wyndham St, Soho** ☎ 2167 8989
⊕ **Central** ⏲ **noon-late**

**Blue Cafe & Bar**
(5, G2) Seeping blue lights and white chairs make this bar an instant zone. Not large, but smooth and snappy with inventive drinks, slow electronica and a zipless crowd sipping cocktails and nibbling on conversation and snacks.
✉ **21 Sharp St E, Causeway Bay** ☎ 2834 5087 ⊕ **Causeway Bay**
⏲ **5pm-2am**

**Brecht's** (5, G4)
Brecht's is very small and fairly unusual. It's an arty kind of place given more to intimate, cerebral conversation than serious raging. The decor is pseudo-German, and includes oversized portraits of such charmers as Mao and Hitler.
✉ **123 Leighton Rd, Causeway Bay** ☎ 2577 9636 ⊕ **Causeway Bay**
⏲ **Sun-Thurs 6pm-2am, Fri-Sat 4pm-4am**

blue – it's cool

**Chapter 3** (6, C3)
Cheerful Boho bar that defies its dungeon setting. It's far less trendy than most bars around here, maintaining a low-key feel with occasional poetry readings and a loyal crowd.
✉ **Amber Lodge, 23 Hollywood Rd (enter from Cochrane St), Boho** ☎ 2526 5566
⊕ **Central** ⏲ **5pm-1am**

**Chemical Suzy** (3, E7)
Cyber-groover hide-out with DJs, snacks (scallops, fishfingers) and enough pop culture signifiers to leave no doubt that Suzy's in the know.
✉ **AWT Centre,**

**2 Austin Ave, Tsim Sha Tsui** ☎ 2736 0087
⊕ **Tsim Sha Tsui**
⏲ **Mon-Sat 6pm-4am, Sun 9pm-4am**

**Club Feather Boa**
(6, C2) Feather Boa is a plush lounge hidden behind gold drapes. The scenario is 'trashy princess meets dilapidated gentleman for a cocktail but ends up drinking bottled beer from a chunky stemmed glass'.
✉ **38 Staunton St, Soho** ☎ 2857 2586 ⊕ **Central**
⏲ **6.30pm-late**

**Gecko** (6, C3)
Relaxed hide-out run by a friendly French sommelier with a penchant for absinthe. The well-hidden DJ mixes good grooves with kooky Parisian tunes.
✉ **15-19 Hollywood Rd (enter from Ezra's Lane off Cochrane St), Boho** ☎ 2526 6559
⊕ **Central** ⏲ **Mon-Thurs 6pm-2am, Fri-Sat 6pm-4am**

## Elvis Spotted in Soho

Hong Kong is not exempt from the global phenomenon that is the Elvis Impersonator. The city's only King clone is one Melvis Kwok, who has been been crooning Elvis tunes on the streets of Hong Kong for the past decade. You might see him saunter by in one of his spangly suits while dining in Soho, or as he croons outside clubs in Lan Kwai Fong. What he loses in the lyrics he gains in gyration. He doesn't force you to pay, but remember, even a dead King has to make a living.

### La Dolce Vita (6, D5)
A buzzing place for post-work brews with room to bar-prop or stand on the terrace and watch the mob crawl by. Gets a bit messy on weekends.
✉ Cosmos Bldg, 9-11 Lan Kwai Fong, Lan Kwai Fong ☎ 2186 1888 🚇 Central
🕐 Sun-Thurs 9am-2am, Fri-Sat 9am-4am

### Le Jardin (6, D4)
Don't imagine a breezy garden – the 'jardin' is an enclosed verandah – but this is still an attractive bar with loads of atmosphere. The mostly expat crowd enjoys itself without getting too boisterous.
✉ 1st fl, Winner Bldg, 10 Wing Wah Lane, Lan Kwai Fong ☎ 2526 2717 🚇 Central
🕐 noon-2am

### Oscar's (6, D5)
High-fashion watering hole and restaurant where you can play 'spot the model'. There's a second location in the World Trade Centre, Causeway Bay (5, E3).
✉ 2 Lan Kwai Fong, Lan Kwai Fong ☎ 2804 6561 🚇 Central
🕐 11am-11pm

### Reef Bar & Cafe (5, H3)
Snug in a strip of motor-cycle workshops, this is an oasis of cocktails, fruit juices and fresh oysters. Take a seat or plant yourself at the bar and watch Swordman the manager shuck 'em.
✉ 13 Caroline Hill Rd, Causeway Bay ☎ 2890 3033 🚇 Causeway Bay
🕐 6-11pm

### Staunton's Wine Bar & Café (6, C2)
Staunton's is swish, cool and on the ball with ice-clinking drinks, an escalator-watching scene and live jazz most evenings. For eats, there's expensive focaccia downstairs and a modern international restaurant upstairs.
✉ 10-12 Staunton St (cnr Shelley St), Soho ☎ 2973 6611 🚇 Central
🕐 9am-midnight

Shuck one at the Reef

## Hotel Bars

### The Bar (3, J5)
For mellow 1940s and 50s jazz, take your smoking jacket along and sip cognac at The Bar. Your fellow tipplers will be serious business types, coutured couples and new money trying to look old. The music starts around 9.30pm.
✉ The Peninsula, cnr Salisbury & Nathan Rds, Tsim Sha Tsui ☎ 2315 3163 🚇 Tsim Sha Tsui 🕐 noon-1am

### Captain's Bar (4, E6)
This is a clubby, suited place that serves ice-cold draught beer in chilled silver mugs. Butlers bring lunch and afternoon-tea buffets and set them up in the bar. This is a good place to talk business, at least until the covers band strikes up at 9pm.
✉ Mandarin Oriental Hotel, 5 Connaught Rd, Central ☎ 2825 4001 🚇 Central 🍴 yes
🕐 11am-2am

### Champagne Bar (4, E12)
Take your fizz in the newly renovated sumptuous surrounds of the Grand Hyatt. Live blues or jazz rings through the bar on most evenings.
✉ Grand Hyatt Hotel, 1 Harbour Rd, Wan Chai ☎ 2588 1234
🕐 9.30pm-1am

### Cyrano's (4, G8)
If you like to get high while you drink, come visit Cyrano's for expert bartenders, Continental meals and live jazz (from 9pm). Change lifts at the 36th floor for a good atrium view on the way up.
✉ 56th fl, Island

Shangri-La Hotel, Supreme Court Rd, Admiralty ☎ 2820 8591 ⊕ Admiralty ⊙ Mon-Sat 7-9am, noon-3pm, 5pm-1.30am; Sun 7-10am, 11.30am-1.30am ⚹

**Felix** (3, J5)
Take a brew with an amazing view at the bar connected to Felix restaurant (p. 81).
✉ The Peninsula, cnr Salisbury & Nathan Rds, Tsim Sha Tsui ☎ 2920 2888 (ext 3188) ⊕ Tsim Sha Tsui ⊙ 6pm-2am

**Hari's** (3, H5)
Tacky or classy? You decide, after you've had a couple of speciality martinis (there are over a dozen to challenge you, including wasabi and garlic). Happy hours are Monday to Saturday 5pm to 9pm and all night Sunday. There's live music nightly: it's covers Monday to Saturday and 'folk classics' Sunday.
✉ Mezzanine, Holiday Inn Golden Mile, 50 Nathan Rd, Tsim Sha Tsui ☎ 2369 3111 (ext 1345) ⊕ Tsim Sha Tsui ⊙ 6pm-2am

**Sky Lounge** (3, J5)
Before you can criticise the departure-lounge feel of this big, long bar you've already started marvelling at the view. Don't take flight: sit down in a scoop chair, sip a drink and scoff international snacks.
✉ 18th fl, Sheraton Hotel & Towers, 20 Nathan Rd, Tsim Sha Tsui ☎ 2369 1111 ⊕ Tsim Sha Tsui ⊙ 2pm-1am ⚹

## Pubs
### Biergarten (3, H6)
This clean modern place has a hits-and-memories jukebox and Bitburger on tap. It's popular with visiting Germans and others who hanker after Black Forest ham, smoked pork loin and schnitzels. This is a nonthreatening place to have a solo beer – on fine days, the front is opened to the street.
✉ 5 Hanoi Rd, Tsim Sha Tsui ☎ 2721 2302 ⊕ Tsim Sha Tsui ⊙ noon-2am

### Bit Point (6, D5)
Owned by the same people as Biergarten, Bit Point and nearby **Schnurrbart** draw fans of German beer who like a rowdy drinking atmosphere. Most beers here are draught pilsners (which you can get in a glass boot if you've got a huge thirst to kick).
✉ 31 D'Aguilar St, Lan Kwai Fong ☎ 2523 7436 ⊕ Central ⊙ Mon-Thurs 11am-1am, Fri-Sat 11am-3am, Sun 6pm-midnight

### Club 1911 (6, C2)
A bar with Art-Nouveau details steeped in colonial nostalgia. If you get the munchies, you can order in food from some of the surrounding eateries. Happy hour is from 5pm to 9pm.
✉ 27 Staunton St, Soho ☎ 2810 6681 ⊕ Central ⊙ Mon-Sat 5pm-midnight

### Delaney's (4, G12)
Delaney's is an incongruously located – yet immensely popular – Irish pub. It's worth the effort to find, as you can order a draught Guinness poured with the care and expertise it deserves. For a change of pace, try Delaney's Ale, a house brew made by the South China Brewing Co. The food is good too – the kitchen goes through 400kg of potatoes a week! Also at 3-7 Prat Ave, Tsim Sha Tsui (3, G6).
✉ 18 Luard Rd, Wan Chai ☎ 2804 2880 ⊕ Wan Chai ⊙ noon-late

### Groovy Mule (4, G11)
Like a coyote bar with less lout and yee haw, but bar antics remain the main draw. Slammers and gyration from the Aussie barstaff keep punters on their barstools, just.
✉ 13 Fenwick St, Wan Chai ☎ 2529 6888 ⊕ Wan Chai ⊙ noon-3am (shows from around 8pm) ⑤ $200, $320 with dinner

### Jungle Pub (4, G12)
Lively drinking cellar which is popular with local Chinese folk who pay more attention to the labels on their beer bottles than

*The Groovy Mule*

those on their clothes. Weekends get rowdy in a nice kind of way.

✉ **Basement, Heng Shun Mansion, 76-82 Jaffe Rd, Wan Chai** ☎ **2529 1828** 🚇 **Wan Chai** ◷ **noon-2am**

### Kangaroo Pub (3, G4)

The infamous Kangaroo is the bane of Australian expats struggling to prove that not all their countrymen are lager louts. This place gets pretty lively, and there are plenty of decent Aussie beers. This is where you come to watch Aussie Rules and rugby on satellite TV.

✉ **1-2nd fl, Daily House, 35 Haiphong Rd, Tsim Sha Tsui** ☎ **2376 0083** 🚇 **Tsim Sha Tsui** ◷ **Mon-Sat 7-9am, noon-3pm, 5pm-1.30am; Sun 7-10am, 11.30am-1.30am**

### Lord Stanley's (2, E4)

Foreigners' bar with all-day breakfast and bar food. The TVs are usually glued to some kind of sport. It's cosy and quiet during the week but the drunken lords have been known to spill out into the street on weekends.

✉ **92a Stanley Main**

*Serious drinkers head for the Vodka Bar*

**St, Stanley** ☎ **2813 9130** 🚇 **Stanley** 🚌 **6, 66, 262 (from Exchange Sq)** ◷ **10am-1am** ♿

### Mes Amis (4, G12)

Easy-going bar in the thick of girly club land. This spot has a good range of wines and a Mediterranean-style snack list. Also at 35 Pottinger St, Central (6, B5); and 15 Ashley Rd, Tsim Sha Tsui (3, H4).

✉ **83 Lockhart Rd, Wan Chai** ☎ **2527 6680** 🚇 **Wan Chai** ◷ **noon-2am**

### Ned Kelly's Last Stand (3, H4)

Ashley Rd has its own little time warp in this tribute to the 19th-century Australian

bushranger and folk hero. A great tradition continues with the Kelly Gang playing Dixieland jazz nightly until 2am. Food is available and there's never a cover charge.

✉ **11a Ashley Rd, Tsim Sha Tsui** ☎ **2376 0562** 🚇 **Tsim Sha Tsui** ◷ **11.30am-2am** ♿

### Petticoat Lane (6, C3)

This salon has a lightning-bolt marble bar and young gentleman portraits on the walls. It's small, subdued and much better suited to chatting than bopping. There's a fair proportion of gay custom though it's popular with straights as well.

✉ **2 Tun Wo Lane, Boho** ☎ **2973 0642** 🚇 **Central** ◷ **Mon-Thurs 10am-2am, Fri-Sat 10am-3am, Sun 5pm-2am**

### Vodka Bar (6, D3)

A clinically cool bar with a glut of vodka choices. The barstaff know their mixes too well, and have been known to be more inebriated than the customers.

✉ **13 Old Bailey St, Soho** ☎ **8208 1313** 🚇 **Central** ◷ **6pm-late**

*Wan Chai's popular Mes Amis*

# SPECTATOR SPORT

## Basketball
The Asian Basketball Association plays some matches in Hong Kong between May and July.

## Cricket
The Hong Kong International Cricket Series is held in late September or early October. This two-day event at the **Hong Kong Stadium** (5, J5; ☎ 2895 7895), 55 Eastern Hospital Rd, So Kan Po, sees teams from Australia, England, India, New Zealand, Pakistan and the West Indies battle it out in a speedy version of the game.

## Horse Racing
Horse racing is Hong Kong's biggest spectator sport. There are about 65 meetings a year at **Happy Valley** (p. 29) and **Sha Tin** (1, D7) in the New Territories. The racing season is from late September to June. Races at Sha Tin are normally held on Saturday from 1pm to 6pm. Splendid Tours offers 'Come Horseracing Tours' to Happy Valley and Sha Tin. See page 55 for details.

*Hong Kong – it's life in the fast lane*

## Rugby
The Seven-A-Side Rugby Tournament, known as the Rugby Sevens, sees teams from all over the world come together in Hong Kong every March or early April for three days of lightning-fast (15min) matches. Even non-rugby fans scramble to get tickets, for there's also plenty of action in the stands. Matches are held at the **Hong Kong Stadium** (5, J5; ☎ 2895 7895), 55 Eastern Hospital Rd, So Kan Po, but getting tickets isn't easy: ask the HKTB (☎ 2508 1234; **e** www.discoverhongkong.com) or the Hong Kong Rugby Football Union (5, H4; ☎ 2504 8311), 1 Stadium Path, So Kan Po.

## Soccer
Hong Kong has a fairly lively amateur soccer league. Games are played on pitches inside the **Happy Valley Racecourse** (5, J2) and at **Mong Kok Stadium**, Flower Market Rd (p. 47). Check the sports sections of the English-language papers or contact the Hong Kong Football Association (☎ 2712 9122), 55 Fat Kwong St, Ho Man Tin, Kowloon, for details.

## Tennis
Several international tennis tournaments are held annually in Hong Kong, the largest in April. The tournaments are held in **Victoria Park**, Causeway Bay (5, E5). Check the local newspapers for details.

# places to stay

With the exception of screechingly lovely high-end joints, Hong Kong's hotels tend to impress only with their numbing sameness or, at the bottom end, with their resemblance to musty cupboards. But with over 35,000 rooms and occupancy usually under 90%, you should find a suitable temporary residence here.

Hong Kong's two high seasons are from March to April and October to November. Outside of these periods, rates tend to drop and happy bonuses can come your way: airport transport, room upgrades, late checkout, free breakfast and complimentary cocktails. If the hotel seems a bit quiet when you arrive, it can be worth asking for an upgrade.

Hong Kong's deluxe hotels are special places, with individual qualities that propel them above the rest. Expect discreet, personalised service, large baths, superlative climate control, extensive cable TV with Internet access, dataports and fax machines.

Top-end hotels are in spiffing locations: they also have smart, comfortable rooms with excellent air-con, inhouse movies and a good variety of room service. Amenities include business facilities, bars and restaurants and fluent English-speaking staff.

Mid-range hotels tend to be generic business/tourist establishments with little to distinguish one from another. Rooms are spacious enough (if you don't plan on playing Twister of an evening), and usually have a bath, limited cable TV and room service.

The majority of Hong Kong's budget digs are in Kowloon, with many on or near Nathan Rd. Though most budget rooms are very small, the places listed here are clean and cheerily shabby rather than grim and grimy. The hotels we've included all have private bathrooms, telephones, TVs and air-con.

## Room Rates

These categories indicate the cost per night of a standard double room:

Deluxe    $2800 and over
Top End   $1200-2799
Mid-Range $800-1199
Budget    $799 and under

Add 3% tax and, usually, a 10% service charge to quoted rates.

# DELUXE

### Grand Hyatt (4, E12)

A recent revamp of the Grand has brought it back from dated dinosaur to a sleek yet sumptuous choice. Each room is technologically charged with cyber-concierge and Internet access, and comfort charged with massive beds and Egyptian cotton sheets.

✉ **1 Harbour Rd, Wan Chai** ☎ 2588 1234; fax 2802 0677 e www .hongkong.hyatt.com
🚇 Wan Chai

*The Grand Hyatt, Wan Chai*

### Inter-Continental Hong Kong (3, K6)

The Inter-Continental tilts at modernity while bowing to colonial traditions such as a fleet of Rolls Royces, uniformed doormen and incessant brass polishing. The impeccable emphasis on service ensures a lot of return leisure and business custom. The restaurants are superb and the foyer bar boasts a beautiful skyline view.

✉ **18 Salisbury Rd, Tsim Sha Tsui** ☎ 2721 1211; fax 2739 4546 e www.hongkong .intercontinental.com
✗ Yu (p. 84)
🚇 Tsim Sha Tsui

### Island Shangri-La

(4, G8) A sterile exterior here conceals swisho sophistication. Personal service is key: staff seem genuinely interested in making your stay pleasant. Nice touches include a library where you can take afternoon tea, an outdoor spa and a 24hr business centre. Half-hourly shuttles service the Convention Centre and the Star Ferry.

✉ **Pacific Place, Supreme Court Rd, Admiralty** ☎ 2877 3838; fax 2521 8742 e www.shangri-la.com
🚇 Admiralty 🚇 Yes

### JW Marriot (4, G9)

Though business-traveller focused, it's also popular with shopoholics who feed their addiction next door at Pacific Place. Well-appointed rooms are drenched in that special hush you get only in top hotels. The cheaper city-side rooms have hill views (rather than air-con infrastructure vistas).

✉ **Pacific Place, 88 Queensway, Admiralty** ☎ 2810 8366; fax 2845 0737 e www.marriot.com
🚇 Admiralty 🚇 Yes

### Mandarin Oriental

(4, E6) This, The Peninsula's Hong Kong Island counterpart, is not architecturally as impressive but has a healthy dose of old-world charm. Styling is sometimes a bit outdated, but the service, food, atmosphere and views are excellent. Rooms have broadband-powered Internet-capable TVs with cordless keyboards for bedside browsing.

✉ **5 Connaught Rd, Central** ☎ 2522 0111; fax 2810 6190 e www .mandarinoriental.com
✗ Vong (p. 73)
🚇 Central 🚇 Yes

### Kids' Perks

Deluxe and top-end hotels know that their smallest guests have special needs. Both business travellers and tourists alike are bringing their children in increasing numbers, and many hotels are reaching out to them. The Peninsula, Island Shangri-La, Mandarin Oriental and many other hotels all hold special programs for children, from art activities to Chinese cooking. Check with individual hotels for their children's services.

*The throne-like Peninsula*

## The Peninsula (3, J5)

Pure colonial elegance awaits in this throne-like structure. Classic European-style rooms boast faxes, DVDs, CD players and marble bathrooms. Newer-wing rooms can offer spectacular harbour views; in the original building, you'll have to make do with interior sumptuousness. See page 22.
✉ cnr Salisbury & Nathan Rds, Tsim Sha Tsui ☎ 2920 2888; fax 2722 4170 e www .peninsula.com ✗ Felix (p. 81), Gaddi's (p. 81), Spring Moon (p. 82) Ⓜ Tsim Sha Tsui

## Renaissance Harbour View (4, E12)

This spectacular hotel adjoins the Convention & Exhibition Centre, ensuring steady suit-and-tie custom. Deal-cutters are catered to with a well-equipped business centre and discreet restaurants. Leisure travellers will appreciate informed concierges and, perhaps, the flashy nightclub. It has the largest of all outdoor pools overlooking the harbour and a kiddies pool as well.
✉ 1 Harbour Rd, Wan Chai ☎ 2802 8888; fax 2802 8833 e www .renaissancehotels.com ✗ Dynasty (p. 85) Ⓜ Wan Chai

## Ritz-Carlton (4, E7)

A truly beautiful hotel with plush rooms that manage to be cosy and incredibly distinguished all at once. Views from harbour-side rooms are – no surprise – breathtaking but the best views might be from the pool: lay back and soak up the skyline. Guests can also enjoy a spa, sauna, steam bath, fully equipped gymnasium and a business centre.
✉ 3 Connaught Rd, Central ☎ 2877 6666; fax 2877 6778 e www.ritzcarlton.com Ⓜ Central Ⓢ Yes

## Special Deals

The best rates at the better hotels tend to come through travel agents and booking services. Also check flight and accommodation packages in advance, or visit the Hotels Association counter at the airport on arrival. The HKTB doesn't book rooms, but hotels advertise special deals via its Web site (e www.discover hongkong.com/hotels). For mid-range and top-end discounted rates try utilising the services of a hotel room consolidator such as Traveller Services (☎ 2375 2222; fax 2375 2233; e www .taketraveller.com).

*This gent heads for The Peninsula; others head for the Grand Hyatt*

# TOP END

### Conrad International

(4, G9) This elegant but unstuffy hotel receives enthusiastic reviews for its attention to business travellers' needs and the foyer bar/lounge is a gossipy/corporate hang-out.
✉ Pacific Place, 88 Queensway, Admiralty ☎ 2521 3838; fax 2521 3888 e www .conradhotels.com ✗ Nicholini's (p. 73) ⊕ Admiralty 🛁 Yes

### Dorsett Seaview Hotel (3, A4)

This hotel does big trade in Chinese group tours. The rooms are fine, but not so delightful that they'll keep you inside: Temple St Night Market and Nathan Rd retail are within easy reach, while the Tin Hau Temple is practically at the front door.
✉ 268 Shanghai St (cnr Public Square St), Yau Ma Tei ☎ 2782 0882; fax 2781 8800 e www.dorsett seaview.com.hk ⊕ Yau Ma Tei 🚌 1, 1A, 2, 6, 6A

### Excelsior Hotel (5, E3)

While the Excelsior can't help but absorb some of the buzz of its retail-mad location, it also maintains a haven-like serenity. It's modern, efficient, arty and trendy with good restaurants, a tennis court, business centre and fab views from harbour-view rooms.
✉ 281 Gloucester Rd, Causeway Bay ☎ 2894 8888; fax 2895 6459 e www.mandarin oriental.com ⊕ Causeway Bay

### Holiday Inn Golden Mile (3, H5)

This businesslike hotel isn't a bad place to base yourself. Rooms are Holiday Inn reliable and there's the brilliant Avenue Restaurant and schmoozy Hari's bar on site.
✉ 50 Nathan Rd (cnr Mody Rd), Tsim Sha Tsui ☎ 2369 3111; fax 2369 8016 e www.goldenmile-hk.holiday-inn.com ⊕ Tsim Sha Tsui

### Hyatt Regency (3, H4)

The towering Hyatt is slightly lower priced than the rest of the deluxe deck and the staff are not at all snooty. Its Chinese Restaurant is justly revered and the Hyatt also wins for having one of the cheesiest bars in Hong Kong: the Chin Chin bar with a shaken-not-stirred 1960s vibe.
✉ 67 Nathan Rd (cnr Peking Rd), Tsim Sha Tsui ☎ 2311 1234; fax 2739 8701 e www .hongkong.hyatt.com ✗ Chinese Restaurant (p. 81) ⊕ Tsim Sha Tsui

### Kowloon Hotel (3, J4)

Part of The Peninsula stable, the Kowloon has a second-string feel, with its comically ostentatious lobby and great views of...the back of The Peninsula Hotel. Nevertheless, the hotel is popular for its unflappable service, decent rooms and the fab dim sum served in the basement restaurant.
✉ 19-21 Nathan Rd (cnr Middle Rd), Tsim Sha Tsui ☎ 2929 2888; fax 2739 9811 e www.peninsula.com ✗ Wan Loong Court (p. 83) ⊕ Tsim Sha Tsui

### Marco Polo Hotel

(3, G3) The lynchpin in the Marco Polo Hotel group's Canton Rd trio: the Marco Polo; the Hong Kong Hotel (3, J3); and the Prince (3, G3). If you stayed in one of these hotels, you could do all your shopping, eating and entertaining in Harbour City and never go outdoors.
✉ 3 Canton Rd, Harbour City, Tsim Sha Tsui ☎ 2113 0888; fax 2113 0022 e www .marcopolohotels.com ⊕ Tsim Sha Tsui

## Serviced Apartments

A mostly post-colonial innovation, there are some excellent serviced apartments springing up. One of the newest is 22 Peel (6, B3; ☎ 2522 3082; fax 2522 2762; e www.shama.com). These chic pads are in the rapidly changing Soho district, a mere tumble down the hill to Central. Ranging from fairly spacious studio flats to two-bedroom apartments, they're all tastefully furnished and exceedingly comfortable. Features include broadband Internet connection, VCD, wine cellar and membership of the nearby New York Fitness Gym (p. 44). Prices range from $16,000 to $36,000/mth.

*A view to die for*

### Metropark Hotel

(2, C3) This flashy new player in the hotel game makes the most of its easterly locale, with 70% of rooms boasting sweeping city-harbour views. Open-plan rooms offer generous workspace and broadband Internet for those who like to mix business with a bit of pleasure. The 'interactive restaurant', where you talk tastes with the chef, is a hit with guests.

✉ 148 Tung Lo Wan Rd, Causeway Bay
☎ 2600 1000; fax 2600 1111  e www.metroparkhotel.com
⊙ Tin Hau

### Regal Airport Hotel

(1, E2) An easy undercover shuffle from the airport terminal, this is a stylish hotel with sleek, comfy rooms, many with futuristic runway views. There's a splashy indoor/outdoor pool complex, half a dozen restaurants and fun games rooms (one for adults, one for kids). Soundproofing ensures the only noise is of your own making.

✉ 9 Cheong Tat Rd, Chek Lap Kok Airport
☎ 2286 8888; fax 2286 8686
e www.regalhotel.com
✗ Cafe Aficionado (p. 79) ⊙ Tung Chung MTR (then bus E31, S51, S61) ▦ A21, E31, S51, S61, S64

### Royal Garden Hotel

(3, G7) Certainly the best-equipped hotel in Tsim Sha Tsui East and one of Hong Kong's most attractive options overall. From the chic blonde wood and chrome lobby to the rooftop sports complex (25m pool, putting green and tennis court with million dollar views), the Royal Garden kicks goals.

✉ 69 Mody Rd, Tsim Sha Tsui East ☎ 2721 5215; fax 2369 9976
e www.rghk.com.hk
✗ Sabatini (p. 83)
⊙ Tsim Sha Tsui

## MID-RANGE

### Empire Hotel Kowloon

(3, F6) The chic new addition to the Empire chain houses i.t. savvy rooms, 'exciting' bathrooms and a truly magnificent indoor swimming pool. It's an easy stroll from here to the Museum of History. Also at 33 Hennessy Rd, Wan Chai (4, G11).

✉ 62 Kimberley Rd, Kowloon ☎ 2685 3000; fax 2685 3685
e ehkresa@asiastandard.com ⊙ Tsim Sha Tsui

### Harbour View International House (Chinese YMCA)

(4, F12) Right next door to the Hong Kong Arts Centre and a mere stroll to the Convention Centre and Wan Chai ferry terminal, this is a great-value choice for its location. Most of the Harbour View's simply furnished but perfectly adequate rooms look out over Victoria Harbour.

✉ 4 Harbour Rd, Wan Chai ☎ 2802 0111; fax 2802 9063  e www.harbour.ymca.org.hk
⊙ Wan Chai

### Kimberley Hotel

(3, F6) It isn't even slightly glam but it's one of the better mid-range hotels in Tsim Sha Tsui, with assured staff and more than adequate rooms and facilities (including golf nets). All the suites have kitchenettes.

✉ 28 Kimberley Rd, Tsim Sha Tsui ☎ 2723 3888; fax 2723 1318
e www.kimberley.com.hk ⊙ Tsim Sha Tsui

### Luk Kwok Hotel

(4, F12) This is a relatively small, not many frills, no harbour views kinda place (though it talks up its city and mountain aspects). Staff are keen and helpful and you're close to Wan Chai's bustle.

✉ 72 Gloucester Rd, Wan Chai ☎ 2866 2166; fax 2866 2622
e www.lukkwokhotel.com ⊙ Wan Chai

### New Astor Hotel

(3, H5) If you want to walk out of your hotel and get a faceful of Hong Kong, this could well be the place to bed down. The New Astor is close to Nathan Rd and right in the epicentre of the shopping mayhem that's Carnarvon and Granville Rds. The rooms are reasonably priced and adequately appointed.

✉ 11 Carnarvon Rd, Tsim Sha Tsui ☎ 2366 7261; fax 2722 7122 e hotel@newastor .com.hk ⊕ Tsim Sha Tsui

### Park Hotel (3, G6)

The Park is busy and congenial with slightly dated rooms of good size. Family suites are also available. The History and Science museums are just over the road; the hustle of Granville Rd is a block away.

✉ 61-65 Chatham Rd S, Tsim Sha Tsui East ☎ 2366 1371; fax 2739 7259 e www.parkhotel.com .hk ⊕ Tsim Sha Tsui

### Royal Pacific Hotel & Towers (3, G2)

Choose between cheaper rooms in the hotel section or flashier rooms in the harbour-facing tower. The location is good: there's a walkway to Kowloon Park, leading onto Nathan Rd and the MTR. The hotel is also connected to the China ferry terminal and close to the shopping at Harbour City.

✉ 33 Canton Rd, Tsim Sha Tsui ☎ 2736 0922; fax 2405 0922 e www .royalpacific.com.hk ⊕ Tsim Sha Tsui

### Royal Plaza Hotel

(2, B2) The plushness is a bit overdone but it has to be admitted that the Plaza is comfortable. We love the heated no-steam bathroom mirrors and the large, loungey pool. Mong Kok KCR is in the adjoining shopping centre – handy if you've business in the New Territories or China.

✉ 193 Prince Edward Rd W, Mong Kok ☎ 2928 8822; fax 2606 0088 e www .royal plaza.com.hk ⊕ Prince Edward 🚆 Mong Kok KCR

### Stanford Hillview Hotel (3, E6)

This is a decent place to swag near the food, fun and all-night dancing of Knutsford Terrace but set far enough back from the Nathan Rd jabber. The rooms are forgettable but fine.

✉ 13-17 Observatory Rd (cnr Knutsford Tce), Tsim Sha Tsui ☎ 2722 7822; fax 2723 3718 e www.stanford-hillview.com ⊕ Tsim Sha Tsui

### Wharney Hotel

(4, G11) The Wharney is noteworthy for its outdoor whirlpool and swimming pool. The so-called Departure Lounge offers nice respite for weary departing guests who are awaiting late-night flights. Plus, there's a bonus feature: cricket fans can pretend they're staying with a smokin' Aussie leg spinner.

✉ 57-73 Lockhart Rd, Wan Chai ☎ 2861 1000; fax 2865 6023 e wharney.gdhotels .net ⊕ Wan Chai 🚆 Yes

*Two views of the Royal Plaza Hotel, Kowloon*

# BUDGET

### Booth Lodge (3, A4)

Run by the Salvation Army, Booth Lodge is appropriately spartan, but clean and comfortable. There is efficient air-con (you can't open the windows), a pleasant café and disabled access. Room rates include breakfast. Note that reception is on the 7th floor.
✉ **11 Wing Sing Lane, Yau Ma Tei** ☎ **2771 9266; fax 2385 1140** **e** **boothlodge. salvation.org.hk**
Ⓜ **Yau Ma Tei**
🚌 **1, 1A, 2, 6, 6A**

### BP International House (3, E3)

The International House is at the top end of Kowloon Park and a short walk to Nathan Rd and Jordan MTR. The rooms are dowdy but comfortable; some of the more expensive rooms have good harbour views. It has bunk rooms, making this a good option if you're travelling with kids or in a group.
✉ **8 Austin Rd, Tsim Sha Tsui** ☎ **2376 1111; fax 2376 1333** **e** **www .megahotels.com.hk**
Ⓜ **Jordan**

### Caritas Bianchi Lodge (3, A4)

Nonprofit lodge with straightforward, fairly spacious rooms. Though it's just off Nathan Rd (and a goalie's throw from Yau Ma Tei MTR) the rear rooms are very quiet and some have views onto Kings Park.
✉ **4 Cliff Rd, Yau Ma Tei** ☎ **2388 1111; fax 2770 6669** **e** **cblresv @bianchi-lodge.com**
Ⓜ **Yau Ma Tei**
🚌 **1, 1A, 2, 6, 6A**

### Caritas Lodge (2, B2)

Caritas Lodge is not as central as its sister hotel but it's cheaper and the linoleum-floored rooms are clean and liveable, if a bit noisy. There's a church, school, community centre and café on site, giving the place a bustling workaday feel.
✉ **134 Boundary St (near Waterloo Rd), Mong Kok** ☎ **2339 3777; fax 2338 2864** **e** **reservationtas-lodge .com** Ⓜ **Prince Edward**
🚌 **1, 1A**

### Garden View International House (YWCA) (4, H5)

Hovering on the border of Central and the Mid-Levels, the Garden View overlooks the zoo and botanic gardens. It's the only place in the area that falls outside the luxury category. Accommodation is plain but comfortable (there's good air-con) and there's an outdoor swimming pool.
✉ **1 MacDonnell Rd, Central** ☎ **2877 3737; fax 2845 6263** **e** **www .ywca.org.hk**
🚌 **12A, minibus 1A**

### Goodrich Hotel (3, C4)

The lobby is plain and the rooms are slightly shabby, but you can't knock Goodrich for value or location: it's right near the Temple St Night Market and Jordan MTR. The quoted rates seem pretty fluid.
✉ **92-94 Woo Sung St, Jordan** ☎ **2332 2020; fax 2332 3138** **e** **goodrichhotel @goodrichhotel.com.hk** Ⓜ **Jordan**

### Nathan Hotel (3, B4)

The Nathan is surprisingly quiet and pleasant; even the cheapest rooms are spacious, clean and serene. It has triples available and is in a good location, right near the Jordan MTR and the Temple St Night Market.
✉ **378 Nathan Rd, Yau Ma Tei** ☎ **2388 5141; fax 2770 4262** **e** **nathan hk@hkstar.com**
Ⓜ **Jordan**

### Salisbury YMCA Hotel (3, J4)

If you manage to book a room here, you'll be rewarded with professional service and excellent exercise facilities. The rooms are comfortable, if somewhat worn, but you won't mind if you keep your eyes on the harbour view. (Gloat factor: the same view is much more expensive at next door's Peninsula.) Family rooms and four-bed dorms are available.
✉ **41 Salisbury Rd, Tsim Sha Tsui** ☎ **2268 7888; fax 2739 9315** **e** **www.ymcahk.org.hk** ✕ **Salisbury Dining Room (p. 82)**
Ⓜ **Tsim Sha Tsui**

### Shamrock Hotel

**(3, D4)** The Shamrock is fantastic value. The beds can be a bit spongy but the rooms are well-sized, clean and airy, and there are excellent kitsch lounges outside the lifts. Jordan MTR is right outside the door and there's a cheap, decent restaurant on site.
✉ **223 Nathan Rd, Tsim Sha Tsui** ☎ **2735 2271; fax 2736 7354** **e** **www.yp.com.hk/ shamrock** Ⓜ **Jordan**

# facts for the visitor

小心摺門．請勿接近

FOLDING DOOR    KEEP CLEAR

*Fire station*

# ARRIVAL & DEPARTURE

Almost all international travellers arrive and depart via Chek Lap Kok airport. Travellers to and from mainland China can use ferry or rail links to Guangzhou and beyond. It's also possible to fly or drive into Macau and catch a ferry from there.

## Air

Hong Kong's sleek Chek Lap Kok airport (1, E2) is built on a huge slab of reclaimed land to the north of hilly Lantau Island.

The airport is connected to the mainland by the 2.2km-long Tsing Ma Bridge, one of the world's longest suspension bridges, linking the islands of Tsing Yi and Ma Wan. Highways and a flashy fast train link the airport with Kowloon and Hong Kong Island.

### Information

General Inquiries
☎ 2181 0000

Flight Information
| | |
|---|---|
| Air Canada | ☎ 2122 8124 |
| Air New Zealand | ☎ 2122 8166 |
| British Airways | ☎ 2216 1088 |
| Cathay Pacific | ☎ 2747 1234 |
| Qantas | ☎ 2822 9060 |
| United Airlines | ☎ 2801 8617 |

Hotel Booking Service
☎ 2286 8688

Left Luggage
☎ 2261 0110

Car Park Information
☎ 2286 0163

### Airport Access

**Train** The Airport Express (☎ 2881 8888; e www.mtr.com.hk) connects Chek Lap Kok with Hong Kong Station ($100) in Central, stopping at Tsing Yi ($60) and Kowloon ($90) along the way. The train takes just 23mins to get to the city and runs every 10mins 6am-1am daily. Vending machines (cash only) dispense tickets at the airport and railway stations en route. You can also use Octopus cards (p. 110).

When leaving Hong Kong, Airport Express stations have check-in counters for flights from Chek Lap Kok, meaning that you can check your bags and obtain a boarding pass for your flight before you've even hit the airport.

**Bus** The Cityflyer airbus (☎ 2873 0818; e www.citybus.com.hk) is an efficient service that takes 35-45mins. Bus No A21 ($33) is best for destinations in Kowloon, with stops along Nathan Rd in Mong Kok, Yau Ma Tei and Tsim Sha Tsui. Bus No A11 ($40) goes to Sheung Wan, Central, Admiralty and Causeway Bay. Change is not given on the bus; tickets can be bought at the booth near the airport bus stand.

Hotel shuttle buses cost $120 and can easily be found in the arrivals hall.

**Taxi** A taxi to the city centre costs around $350 ($250 to Kowloon). Taxi stands are well signposted.

## Bus

Several transport companies in Hong Kong offer bus services to Guangzhou, Shenzhen and other destinations in Guangdong Province. These include Eternal East (☎ 2723 2923), CTS (☎ 2789 5401), Global Express (☎ 2375 0099) and Airport Chinalink (☎ 9747 1202).

## Train

The Kowloon–Guangzhou express train ($190, 182km, 2hrs), departs from the Kowloon-Canton Railway (KCR) terminal (4, E9) in Hung Hom, Kowloon. There are seven departures daily. Tickets can be booked up to seven days in advance at KCR stations in Hung Hom, Mong Kok, Kowloon Tong and Sha Tin, from China Travel Service agents or over the phone (☎ 2947 7888).

There is a direct rail link between Kowloon, Shanghai and Beijing. Trains to Beijing (via Guangzhou, Changsha, Wuchang and Zhengzhou) leave on alternate days, take around 30hrs and cost $574/934/1191 hard sleeper/ soft sleeper/deluxe sleeper. The trains to Shanghai (via Guangzhou and Hangzhou) also leave on alternate days, take 29hrs and cost $508/825/1039. There is also one departure daily to Zhaoqing via Foshan. Call ☎ 2947 7888 for further information and to book tickets.

## Boat

Services to/from Macau run virtually 24hrs. Boats depart from the Macau ferry terminal (4, B3) at the Shun Tak Centre, Sheung Wan, and the China ferry terminal (3, G2), Kowloon. Tickets ($130 from Hong Kong Island, $120 from Kowloon; higher prices at night) can be bought at the terminals, or by phoning ☎ 2859 3333. It's advisable to book ahead for week-end trips.

Jet catamarans and hovercraft leave from the China ferry terminal to destinations in neighbouring Guangdong Province, including Huizhou, Nanhai, Shenzhen, Zhuhai and Guangzhou.

Turbo Cat (☎ 2921 6688) has two trips daily to East River Guangzhou (the Guangzhou Economic Zone).

The China ferry terminal also has daily morning jet boats to Wuzhou in Guangxi Province, from where you can link up with buses to Guilin, Yangshuo and Nanning.

## Travel Documents

### Passport
Must be valid for one month from date of entry.

### Visa
Not required for citizens of the UK (up to six months), Commonwealth countries and most Western European countries (up to three months) and Japan and South Africa (up to one month). Others should check visa regulations before leaving home.

### Return/Onward Ticket
A return ticket may be required.

## Customs

Firearms are strictly controlled and special permits are needed to import them. Meat, plant and tex-tile products are restricted. Pirated copies of computer software or music are banned: this law is aimed at traders but individuals should still be careful.

The duty-free allowance for visitors is 200 cigarettes (or 50 cigars or 250g tobacco) and 1L of alcohol. Apart from these limits there are few other import taxes, so you can bring in reasonable quantities of almost anything.

## Departure Tax

Hong Kong levies a departure tax of $80 per person, which is usually prepaid when you buy your air ticket.

# GETTING AROUND

Hong Kong is small and crowded, and public transport is the only practical way to move people. The ultra-modern Mass Transit Railway (MTR) subway is the quickest way to get to most urban destinations. The bus system is extensive and as efficient as traffic allows but it can be bewildering for short-stay travellers. Ferries are fast and economical and come with harbour views.

## Travel Passes

The rechargeable Octopus card allows travel on the MTR, Airport Express, KCR East Rail, most cross-harbour bus routes, all outlying island routes of Hong Kong Ferry Co (HKF) ferries and some suburban buses. The card costs $150, which includes a $50 refundable deposit and $100 worth of travel. It's available from MTR, Airport Express and KCR East Rail stations and certain HKF terminals.

Transport passes aimed at tourists are not good value, as you are charged for a 'souvenir' card to take home with you.

## Bus

KMB (☎ 2745 4466; e www.kmb .com.hk) services Kowloon and the New Territories, while Citybus (☎ 2873 0818; e www.citybus .com.hk) covers Hong Kong Island. New World First Buses span the whole territory. Most buses run from about 6am-midnight. Fares range from $2.50-30, though a typical trip will cost around $5. Payment is made by Octopus card (see Travel Passes earlier) or by depositing cash into a fare box upon entry; no change is given.

Central's most important bus terminal is on the ground floor under Exchange Square (4, D5).

From here you can catch buses to Aberdeen, Repulse Bay, Stanley and other destinations on the southern side of Hong Kong Island. In Kowloon, the Star Ferry bus terminal (3, J3) has buses up Nathan Rd and to the KCR terminal.

Figuring out which bus you want can be difficult although it's useful to know that any bus number ending with the letter M (51M, 68M etc) goes to an MTR station and that buses with an X are express. Bus Nos 121 and 122 are night buses that operate through the Cross-Harbour Tunnel every 15mins from 12.45am-5am.

### Minibus

Known as Public Light Buses, minibuses are 16-seater, cream-coloured with a green or red roof or stripe down the side. In Tsim Sha Tsui No 1 runs from the Star Ferry bus terminal to Tsim Sha Tsui East every 5mins from 7am-10pm ($2.50). On Hong Kong Island, a useful route is from Edinburgh Place (near the Star Ferry terminal) to the Peak.

The price to the final destination is displayed on a card propped up in the window. You pay when you get on and no change is given.

## Train

### Mass Transit Railway (MTR)

The MTR (☎ 2881 8888; e www .mtr.com.hk) is clean, fast and safe and transports around three million people daily. Travel costs from $4-13. Trains run every 2-4mins, 6am-1am daily on four lines (see inside front cover). Avoid rush hours if possible: 7-9.30am and 5-7pm.

Everything on the MTR is automated, from the ticket vending machines to the turnstiles. Ticket machines take $10, $5, $2 and $1 notes and 50c pieces, and give change; a handful of machines take $20 notes. The easiest way to travel is with an Octopus card (see Travel Passes earlier).

## Kowloon-Canton Railway (KCR)

The KCR (☎ 2602 7799; e www .kcrc.com) is a single-line commuter railway running from Kowloon to the mainland China border at Lo Wu. The KCR is a quick way to get up to the New Territories. The half-hour ride to Sheung Shui costs $9 ($18 for 1st class), while the 45min trip to Lo Wu costs $33 ($66). A double-decker train also speeds from Hung Hom nonstop to Lo Wu (30mins, $66).

## Tram

Hong Kong Island's double-decker trams (p. 21) are not fast but are heaps of fun. For a flat fare of $2 (dropped in a box beside the driver when you leave) you can rattle along as far as you like. Trams operate 6am-1am, and run every 2-7mins. Try to get a seat at the front window upstairs to enjoy a first-class view.

There are eight tram routes: Kennedy Town–Causeway Bay, Kennedy Town–Happy Valley, Kennedy Town–North Point, Kennedy Town–Shau Kei Wan, Western Market–Causeway Bay, Shau Kei Wan–Happy Valley, Western Market–Shau Kei Wan and Whitty Street–North Point.

The Peak Tram (p. 17) departs from Garden Rd, near the northwestern corner of Hong Kong Park, Admiralty (4, G6). It runs to Victoria Peak every 10-15mins 7am-midnight. The one-way/return fare is $20/30, children 3-11 $6/9, seniors $7/14.

## Ferry

There are four Star Ferry routes, but by far the most popular is the one running between Tsim Sha Tsui (3, K3) and Central (4, D7). The trip takes 7mins and fares are $1.70 (lower deck) and $2.20 (upper deck), free for seniors. Star Ferries also link Tsim Sha Tsui with Wan Chai, and Central with Hung Hom and Discovery Bay (Lantau Island). See page 19 for more information.

The Hong Kong Ferry (HKF) company connects Hong Kong Island to Kowloon and the New Territories, and Central to Tsim Sha Tsui East. HKF also services outlying islands, including Lantau, Cheung Chau, Peng Chau and Lamma. Departures are from piers 6 and 7 (4, C6) in Central.

## Taxi

Hong Kong taxis are a bargain in comparison to other big-city cabs, though the MTR can often be better value and quicker. The flag fall for taxis in Hong Kong and Kowloon is $15 for the first 2km and $1.40 for every additional 200m.

## Car

Driving a car in crowded Hong Kong brings little joy. The traffic often slows to a crawl and finding parking is a nightmare.

### Road Rules

Driving is on the left side of the road. Seat belts must be worn by the driver and all front-seat passengers in taxis and by front- and back-seat passengers in private cars.

The speed limit is 50km/h in urban areas and up to 100km/h on highways. The blood alcohol limit is 0.05%. Drivers are not permitted to use hand-held mobile phones while driving.

### Rental

Many businesspeople hire cars with drivers – even if you're stuck in traffic, you can skim through notes and make phone calls and you don't have to worry about parking. Ace Hire Car (☎ 2893 0541), 16 Min Fat St, Happy Valley, charges $160/hr for a Mercedes Benz with driver. Most hotels will also be able to organise a car for you.

If you're hellbent on driving yourself, Avis (5, G3; ☎ 2890 6988), 93 Leighton Rd, Causeway Bay, charges around $580/day for a compact car. Drivers must be at least 25 years of age.

### Driving Licence & Permit

Anyone over the age of 18 with a valid driving licence from their home country or an international driving licence can drive in Hong Kong for up to 12 months.

### Motoring Organisations

The Hong Kong Automobile Association (3, B4; ☎ 2739 5273) is at 391 Nathan Rd, Yau Ma Tei.

# PRACTICAL INFORMATION

## Climate & When to Go

October-November and April-May are the best times to visit. Temperatures are moderate, and there's a good chance of clear skies and sun. December-March tends to see a lot of rain, and during June-September the sweltering heat and humidity make for sweaty sightseeing.

Hong Kong hotels have two high seasons: March-April and October-November. You can find substantial discounts on accommodation outside these peak periods.

Travel in and out of Hong Kong can be difficult during Chinese New Year, which falls around late January/early February.

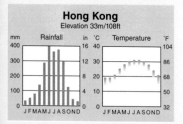

**Hong Kong**
Elevation 33m/108ft

## Tourist Information

### Tourist Information Abroad

The Hong Kong Tourism Board (HKTB) is responsible for marketing Hong Kong as a tourism destination worldwide and enriching visitors' experiences. This efficient and friendly organisation produces reams of useful pamphlets and publications and its website (e www .discoverhongkong.com) is a good point of reference. HKTB overseas offices include:

Australia
L4, Hong Kong House, 80 Druitt St, Sydney, NSW 2000 (☎ 02-9283 3083; e sydwwo@hktb.com)

Canada
3rd fl, Hong Kong Trade Centre, 9 Temperance St, Toronto, Ontario M5H 1Y6 (☎ 416-366 2389; e yyzwwo@ hktb.com)

New Zealand
L2, 99 Queen St, Auckland (☎ 09-307 2580; e aukwwo@hktb.com)

UK
6 Grafton St, London W1S 4EQ (☎ 020-7533 7100; e lonwwo@hktb.com)

## USA

Suite 1640, 401 N Michigan Ave, Chicago, IL 60611 (☎ 312-329 1828; e chiwwo@hktb.com);

2nd fl, 115 E 54th St, New York, NY 10022-4512 (☎ 212-421 3382; e nycwwo@hktb.com);

Suite 2050, 10940 Wilshire Blvd, Los Angeles, CA 90024-3915 (☎ 310-208 0233; e laxwwo@hktb.com);

130 Montgomery St, San Francisco, CA 94104 (☎ 415-781 4587; e sfowwo@hktb.com)

### Local Tourist Information

There are HKTB centres at Chek Lap Kok airport (1, E2); Star Ferry Concourse, Tsim Sha Tsui (3, K3); and at The Center, Central (4, D4). You can also call the HKTB Visitor Hotline (multilingual) on ☎ 2508 1234 from 8am-6pm.

## Consulates

Hong Kong is one of the world's most consulate-clogged cities.

### Australia

23rd & 24th fl, Harbour Centre, 25 Harbour Rd, Wan Chai (4, E13; ☎ 2827 8881)

### Canada

11th-14th fl, Tower One, Exchange Sq, 8 Connaught Pl, Central (4, D6; ☎ 2810 4321)

### New Zealand

6501 Central Plaza, 18 Harbour Rd, Wan Chai (4, F13; ☎ 2525 5044)

### South Africa

27th fl, Great Eagle Centre, 23 Harbour Rd, Wan Chai (4, E13; ☎ 2577 3279)

### UK

1 Supreme Court Rd, Admiralty (4, G8; ☎ 2901 3000)

### USA

26 Garden Rd, Central (4, G6; ☎ 2523 9011)

## Money

### Currency

The local currency is the Hong Kong dollar ($ throughout this book). The dollar is divided into 100c. Notes are issued in denominations of $20, $50, $100, $500 and $1000. Coins are issued in denominations of 10c, 20c, 50c, $1, $2, $5 and $10.

### Travellers Cheques

Most banks cash travellers cheques for a fee. The best deal is probably the Dao Heng Bank, which charges a flat rate of $20 per cheque. The Hongkong and Shanghai Bank charges 0.375% of the total amount (minimum charge $50), Standard Chartered tacks on a 0.375% (minimum $100) commission and Hang Seng charges $60. Licensed moneychangers don't levy a commission but give a lower rate of exchange.

### Credit Cards

The most widely accepted credit cards in Hong Kong are American Express, Diners Club, JCB, Master-Card and Visa. For 24hr card cancellations or assistance, call:

American Express
☎ 2811 6122

Diners Club
☎ 2860 1888

JCB
☎ 2366 7211

MasterCard
☎ 2598 8038

Visa
☎ 2810 8033

### ATMs

You will rarely have to search far to find an ATM. International travellers will be able to withdraw funds from their home accounts using just about any cashpoint in town. Refreshingly, most banks don't pilfer a fee for the service.

### Changing Money

Licensed moneychangers, such as Thomas Cook and Chequepoint, are abundant in tourist areas and keep extensive hours. There is no commission, but the exchange rates offered are equivalent to a 5% commission. Banks have marginally better exchange rates.

## Tipping

Feel no obligation to tip taxi drivers, but tip hotel porters at least $10. If you make use of airport porters, $2 a suitcase is normally expected. Hotels and restaurants usually add a 10% service charge. In fancy restaurants customers may tip an extra 5-10% for good service.

## Discounts

Children and seniors are generally offered half-price transport and attractions but family tickets are not usually available. The HKTB offers a $30 museum pass – this gets you into six museums in one week.

### Student & Youth Cards

If you're a student or under 27, you can apply for an STA Youth Card; students under 27 also qualify for an International Student Identity Card (ISIC). Both cards entitle you to discounts on airfares, trains and museums – inquire at your campus.

## Travel Insurance

A policy that covers theft, loss, medical expenses and compensation for cancellation or delays in your travel arrangements is highly recommended. If items are lost or stolen, make sure you get a police report straight away otherwise your insurer might not pay up.

## Opening Hours

Business hours are Mon-Fri 9am-5pm, and Sat 9am-noon. Many offices close for lunch between 1-2pm. Stores that cater to the tourist trade keep longer hours, but almost nothing opens before 9am and many stores don't open until 10am or 11am. Even tourist-related businesses shut down by 10pm. Most banks, post offices, shops and attractions are closed on public holidays; restaurants usually open Sundays.

## Public Holidays

| | |
|---|---|
| 1 Jan | New Year's Day |
| Jan/Feb | Chinese New Year (3 days) |
| Late Mar/Apr | Easter (3 days) |
| Early April | Ching Ming |
| Late April | Buddha's Birthday |
| 1 May | Labour Day |
| June | Dragon Boat/ Tuen Ng Festival |
| 1 July | Hong Kong SAR Establishment Day |
| 1 Oct | National Day |
| Early Oct | Chinese Mid-Autumn Festival |
| Late Oct | Cheung Yeung |
| 25 Dec | Christmas Day |
| 26 Dec | Boxing Day |

## Time

Hong Kong Standard Time is 8hrs ahead of GMT/UTC and summer/daylight-savings time isn't practised. At noon in Hong Kong it's:

11pm the previous day in New York
8pm the previous day in Los Angeles
4am in London
noon in Singapore, Manila and Perth
2pm in Melbourne and Sydney

## Electricity

The standard voltage is 220V, 50Hz AC. Outlet shapes often vary, but inexpensive plug adaptors are widely available.

## Weights & Measures

Although the international metric system (p. 122) is in official use, traditional Chinese weights and measures are still common. At local markets, items are sold by the *leung* (37.8g) and the *gan* (catty; about 600g). There are 16 *leung* to the *gan*.

## Post

On Hong Kong Island, the General Post Office (GPO) is just east of Ferry Pier (4, D6). It opens Mon-Fri 9am-5pm, Sat 9am-noon, Sunday 8am-2pm. In Kowloon, convenient post offices are at 10 Middle Rd (3, J5), and in Albion Plaza basement (3, G5). Most post offices have stamp vending machines outside, useful after hours. The postal services inquiry number is ☎ 2921 2222.

Allow five days for delivery of letters, postcards and aerogrammes to the UK, USA and Australia. Speedpost reduces delivery time by about half. Airmail letters and postcards are $2.40 (to Asia except Japan) and $3 (elsewhere) for the first 20g; and $1.20 and $1.30 respectively for each additional 10g. Aerogrammes are $2.30 for both zones.

## Telephone

All calls made within Hong Kong are local calls and therefore free, except at public pay phones, which cost $1 for 5mins. You can place an International Direct Dialling (IDD) call from most phone boxes, but you'll probably need a phonecard, which can be bought at PCCW shops (☎ 2883 3938; **e** www.pccw.com) and convenience stores. Other, often cheaper phonecards such as Chi-Tel cards are available at convenience stores. Lonely Planet's ekno Communication Card (**e** www.ekno.lonelyplanet.com) provides competitive international calls, messaging services and free email.

### Mobile Phones

Hong Kong boasts the world's highest per-capita usage of mobile telephones and pagers. Any GSM-compatible phone can be used in Hong Kong.

PCCW shops rent and sell mobile phones, SIM cards and phone accessories. SIM cards cost $200, network rental is $200/wk and local calls cost $2.20/min. These phones are IDD compatible but there's an extra charge if you need a roaming service to take into China. Handset rentals are available for an extra $250/wk.

### Country Code

| | |
|---|---|
| Hong Kong | ☎ 852 |

### Useful Numbers

| | |
|---|---|
| Local Directory Inquiries | ☎ 1081 |
| International Directory Inquiries | ☎ 10013 |
| International Fax Dialling Code | ☎ 002 |
| International Operator | ☎ 10010 |
| International Operator (credit-card calls) | ☎ 10011 |
| Reverse-Charge (collect) | ☎ 10010 |
| Time & Weather | ☎ 18501 |

### International Direct Dial Codes

Dial ☎ 001 then:

| | |
|---|---|
| Australia | ☎ 61 |
| Canada | ☎ 1 |
| Rest of China | ☎ 86 |
| Japan | ☎ 81 |
| New Zealand | ☎ 64 |
| South Africa | ☎ 27 |
| UK | ☎ 44 |
| USA | ☎ 1 |

## Digital Resources

### Internet Service Providers

Local ISPs include PCCW's Netvigator (☎ 1833 833; @ premserv@netvigator.com) and HKNet (☎ 2110 2288; @ info@hknet.com). America Online's customer service number is ☎ 2892 2627.

### Internet Cafés

If you can't access the Internet from your hotel, Hong Kong has plenty of Internet access options:

Cyber Cafe
7 Lock Rd , Tsim Tsa Shui (3, H4; ☎ 2537 8778)

Hong Kong Central Library
66 Causeway Rd, Causeway Bay (5, F5; ☎ 3150 1234) free access

Kublai's
3rd fl, One Capital Pl, 18 Luard Rd, Wan Chai (4, F12; ☎ 2529 9117)

Pacific Coffee Company
1st fl, International Finance Centre, 1 Harbour View St (4, D6; ☎ 2868 5100); also most other shopping centres

Rainbow Online
Basement, 478 Nathan Rd, Yau Ma Tei (3, A4; ☎ 2374 1723)

### Useful Sites

The Lonely Planet website (@ www.lonelyplanet.com) links to Hong Kong sites via Subwwway and covers travel news at Scoop. Other useful sites include:

Hong Kong government information
@ www.info.gov.hk

Hong Kong Tourist Board
@ www.discoverhongkong.com

South China Morning Post (news)
@ www.scmp.com.hk

Telephone Directories
@ www.pccw.com

Totally Hong Kong (lifestyle)
@ www.totallyhk.com

## Doing Business

The Hong Kong Trade Development Council (TDC; @ www.tdctrade.com) promotes Hong Kong as a trading and manufacturing partner for foreign businesses. Its office within the Convention & Exhibition Centre (4, E12; ☎ 2584 4333) includes a library. Other business sources are the Hong Kong Trade Department (2, B2; ☎ 2392 2922), Trade Department Tower, 700 Nathan Rd, Mong Kok; and the Hong Kong Trade & Industry Department (3, H3; ☎ 2737 2208; @ www.tid.gov.hk), 14th fl, Ocean Centre, Tsim Sha Tsui. Females can utilise the Women Business Owners Club (☎ 2541 0446).

For office and staff hire contact the Asia Pacific Business Centre (4, F8; ☎ 2530 8888; @ asiapac@winclient.com), 2207-9 Tower 2, Lippo Centre, Admiralty; or the Central Executive Business Centre (4, E5; ☎ 2841 7888), 11th fl, Central Bldg, Central.

For translation and interpretation services try Polyglot Translations (6, B2; ☎ 2851 7232; @ polyglot@hkstar.com), 14b, Time Centre, Central.

## Newspapers & Magazines

The local English-language dailies are the South China Morning Post and the Hong Kong Standard (Mon-Sat). The mouthpiece China Daily prints a Hong Kong edition. Asian editions of the Asian Wall Street Journal, USA Today and the International Herald Tribune are printed in Hong Kong. All are available at Star Ferry terminals and hotel bookshops.

## Radio

Hong Kong's popular English-language radio stations are RTHK

Radio 3 (567AM, 1584AM, 97.9FM, 106.8FM); RTHK Radio 4 (classical music, 98.9FM); RTHK Radio 6 (BBC World Service 675AM); Commercial Radio (864AM); Metro News (1044AM); Hit Radio (99.7FM); FM Select (104FM); and Quote AM (alternative and dance music, 864AM). The *South China Morning Post* publishes a daily guide to radio programs.

## TV

The two English-language stations are TVB Pearl (channel 3) and ATV World (channel 4). The program schedule is listed daily in the *South China Morning Post* and in a weekly Sunday liftout.

# Photography & Video

Any photographic accessory you could possibly need is available in Hong Kong.

Hong Kong subscribes to the PAL video standard used in Australia, New Zealand, UK and most of Europe. It's incompatible with SECAM and NTSC.

# Health

## Immunisations

There are no specific vaccination requirements for Hong Kong or Macau. For Guangzhou and southern China a yellow fever vaccination is needed if you are coming from an infected area.

## Precautions

In general, health conditions in Hong Kong are good. The government insists that Hong Kong's tap water is perfectly safe to drink. Bottled water is widely available.

Practice the usual precautions when it comes to sex; condoms are widely available.

## Insurance & Medical Treatment

It's advisable to take out travel insurance to cover the cost of any medical treatment you may need. Medical care in Hong Kong is of a high standard though public hospital facilities are stretched. Private hospital treatment is fairly expensive, but not exorbitant and you'll have less of a wait for treatment.

## Medical Services

The general inquiry number for hospitals is ☎ 2300 6555. Some hospitals with 24hr accident and emergency departments include:

Hong Kong Central (private)
  1b Lower Albert Rd, Central, Hong Kong Island (6, E5; ☎ 2522 3141)

Queen Elizabeth Hospital (public)
  30 Gascoigne Rd, Yau Ma Tei, Kowloon (3, A6; ☎ 2958 8888)

Queen Mary Hospital (public)
  102 Pok Fu Lam Rd, Pok Fu Lam, Hong Kong Island (2, D2; ☎ 2855 3111)

## Dental Services

Private dental clinics can be found throughout Hong Kong; hospitals also offer emergency dental services. To find a dentist nearby, ask your hotel or call the Dental Council (☎ 2873 5862).

## Pharmacies

Mannings and Watson's are pharmacy chains with branches across Hong Kong. The hospitals listed above have dispensing chemists on duty 24hrs.

## Traditional Practitioners

Traditional Chinese medicine is extremely popular in Hong Kong, both as a preventative and curative. See page 67 for more information.

## Toilets

You need a strong bladder in Hong Kong – the city suffers from a scarcity of public toilets. Seek out toilets in malls, hotels, fast-food outlets and department stores. Bring your own toilet paper.

## Safety Concerns

Hong Kong is extremely safe for visitors. As you go further north in Kowloon and into the New Territories, the crime rate increases, but criminals would still rather target locals than visitors. In any event, it's unwise to flash valuables and you should remain alert just in case.

### Lost Property

Each public transport service manages its own lost property:

| | |
|---|---|
| Citybus | ☎ 2873 0818 |
| Hongkong Ferry | ☎ 2815 6063 |
| Hongkong Tramways | ☎ 2548 7102 |
| KCR | ☎ 2602 7799 |
| KMB | ☎ 2745 4466 |
| MTR | ☎ 2881 8888 |
| New World First Bus | ☎ 2136 8888 |
| Peak Tramways | ☎ 2522 0922 |
| Star Ferry | ☎ 2366 2576 |

### Keeping Copies

Make photocopies of all important documents, keep some with you, separate from the originals, and leave a copy at home. You can also store details of documents in Lonely Planet's free online Travel Vault (**e** www.ekno.lonelyplanet .com).

## Emergency Numbers

| | |
|---|---|
| Ambulance | ☎ 999 |
| Fire | ☎ 999 |
| Police | ☎ 999 |
| Police (non-emergency) | ☎ 2527 7177 |
| Rape Crisis Line | ☎ 2375 5322 |

## Women Travellers

The experience of most women travellers is that Hong Kong is a safe city. That said, it's still important to take care, especially if alone at night. Be wary of agencies seeking women to work as models and film extras; these agencies can be fronts for prostitution.

Tampons are widely available but there's not a lot of variety – most Hong Kong women use sanitary pads. The contraceptive pill is available by prescription.

## Gay & Lesbian Travellers

Despite the 1991 removal of criminal penalties for homosexual acts between those over 18 years old, people remain fairly conservative about homosexuality. Horizons (☎ 2815 9268) is an advice service for gays, lesbians and bisexuals. See page 91 for information and entertainment listings.

## Senior Travellers

Overall, Hong Kong is safe and comfortable, however some may have difficulty with hills or steps. Senior discounts are available; see page 114. The Hong Kong Society for the Aged (4, F13; ☎ 2511 2235), Rm1601, Tung Sun Commercial Centre, 194 Lockhart Rd, Wan Chai, deals with issues relating to the elderly.

## Disabled Travellers

Disabled people will have to cope with MTR stairs, crowded footpaths and steep hills. People whose sight, hearing or walking ability is impaired must be extremely cautious of Hong Kong's crazy drivers. On the other hand, taxis are everywhere and most buildings have lifts. Wheelchairs can negotiate most of the ferries and some newer buses.

Some hotels have specially designed rooms for disabled guests, and Chek Lap Kok airport has good facilities for special-needs passengers: a free porter service, ramps, and lifts with audible indicators. The HKTB publishes a booklet listing hotels, attractions and shopping centres that cater to wheelchair visitors. The Joint Council for the Physically and Mentally Disabled (☎ 2864 2931) might be able to help.

## Language

Hong Kong's two official languages are English and Cantonese. However, around 70% of the population of China speaks Mandarin, the official language of the People's Republic of China (PRC). While Cantonese is used in Hong Kong in everyday life, English is still the primary language of commerce, banking and international trade, and is also used in the higher law courts.

Since the handover, there has been a sharp rise in Mandarin-speaking tourists and some locals are now learning Mandarin instead of English as their second language. For a Cantonese native speaker, Mandarin is far easier to learn than English. Still, short-term English-speaking visitors can get along fine in Hong Kong without a word of Cantonese, especially in the tourist zones. Street signs and public transport information are presented in both English and Cantonese, so there's no problem getting around. However, in the back streets, markets and non-touristy restaurants, conversing with locals will be a little more difficult.

### Tones & Romanisation

Chinese languages have many homonyms (sound-alike words). What distinguishes the meaning of these words are changes in a speaker's pitch (tones) and the context of the word within the sentence. Attempting to explain the tonal system (or the various Romanisation systems used to render Cantonese script into a form Westerners can read and pronounce) would require a disordinate amount of space. The words and phrases included here therefore use a simplified system of Romanisation and are not marked for tones.

For an in-depth guide to Cantonese – with loads of useful information on grammar, tones and pronunciation, together with a comprehensive phrase list – get a copy of Lonely Planet's *Cantonese phrasebook*.

### Pronouns

| | |
|---|---|
| I | ngoh |
| you | nei |
| he/she/it | kui |
| we/us | ngoh dei |
| you (plural) | nei dei |
| they/them | kui dei |

### Basics

| | |
|---|---|
| Hello, how are you? | nei ho? |
| I'm fine. | ngoh gei ho |
| Good morning. | jo san |
| Goodbye. | baai baai |
| Goodnight. | jo tau |
| Thanks. (for a gift or special favour) | do je |
| You're welcome. | m sai haak hei |
| Excuse me. | m goi |
| I'm sorry. | dui m jue |

### Small Talk

| | |
|---|---|
| What is your surname? (polite) | cheng man gwai sing? |
| My surname is ... | siu sing ... |
| My name is ... | ngoh giu ... |

| | |
|---|---|
| This is Mr/Mrs/Ms (Lee). | ni wai hai (lei) sin saang/taai taai/siu je |
| Glad to meet you. | ho go hing ying sik nei |
| Can you please help me take a photo? | ho m ho yi bong ngoh ying jeung seung a? |
| Is it OK to take a photo? | ho m ho yi ying seung a? |

## Language Difficulties

| | |
|---|---|
| Do you speak English? | nei sik m sik gong ying man a? |
| Do you understand? | nei ming m ming a? |
| I understand. | ngoh ming |
| I don't understand. | ngoh m ming |
| Can you repeat that please? | cheng joi gong yat chi? |
| What is this called? | ni goh giu mat ye a? |

## Getting Around

| | |
|---|---|
| Go straight ahead. | yat jik hui |
| left/right | joh bin/yau bin |
| airport | gei cheung |
| bus stop | ba si jaam |
| ferry pier | siu lin ma tau |
| subway station | dei tit jaam |
| information centre | sun man chue |
| north | bak |
| south | naam |
| east | dung |
| west | sai |
| I'd like to go to ... | ngoh seung hui ... |
| Does this (bus) go to ...? | ni ga (ba si) hui m hui ... a? |
| How much is the fare? | gei doh chin a? |
| I want to get off at ... | ngoh seung hai ... lok che? |
| Stop here please. (taxi, minibus) | m goi, ni do yau lok |

| | |
|---|---|
| Where is the ..., please? | cheng man ... hai bin do a? |
| Is it far? | yuen m yuen a? |
| Please write down the address for me. | m goi se goh dei ji bei ngoh |

## Accommodation

| | |
|---|---|
| Do you have any rooms? | yau mo fong a? |
| I'd like a (single/ double) room. | ngoh seung yiu yat goh (daan/seung) yan fong |
| I'd like a quiet room. | ngoh seung yiu yat gaan jing di ge fong |
| How much per night? | gei doh chin yat maan a? |

## Eating & Drinking

| | |
|---|---|
| restaurant | chaan teng |
| bar | jau ba |
| food court/street | sik gaai |
| delicious | ho ho me |
| I'm a vegetarian. | ngoh hai so sik ge |
| Do you have an English menu? | yau mo ying man chaan paai a? |
| Can you recommend any dishes? | yau mat ye ho gaai siu a? |
| I'd like the set menu, please. | ngoh yiu goh to chaan |
| Please bring me (a knife and fork). | m goi loh (yat foo do cha) bei ngoh |
| Please bring the bill. | m goi maai daan |

## Shopping

| | |
|---|---|
| How much is this? | ni goh gei doh chin a? |
| That's very expensive. | ho gwai |
| Can you reduce the price? | peng di dak m dak a? |
| I'm just looking. | ngoh sin tai yat tai |

## Days & Numbers

| day | yat |
|---|---|
| week | sing kei |
| today | gam yat |
| tomorrow | ting yat |
| yesterday | kam yat |

| 0 | ling |
|---|---|
| 1 | yat |
| 2 | yi (or leung) |
| 3 | saam |
| 4 | sei |
| 5 | ng |
| 6 | luk |
| 7 | chat |
| 8 | baat |
| 9 | gau |
| 10 | sap |
| 11 | sap yat |
| 12 | sap yi |
| 20 | yi sap |
| 21 | yi sap yat |
| 100 | yat baak |
| 1000 | yat chin |
| 10,000 | yat maan |
| 100,000 | sap maan |
| 1,000,000 | yat baak maan |
| 10,000,000 | yat chin maan |
| 100,000,000 | yat yik |

## Health

| I'm sick. | ngoh yau beng |
|---|---|
| My friend is sick. | ngoh pang yau yau beng |
| I need a doctor. | ngoh yiu tai yi sang |
| It hurts here. | ni do m sue fuk |
| I have asthma. | ngoh haau chuen |
| I have diarrhoea. | ngoh to ngoh |
| I'd like to see a female doctor. | ngoh yiu wan yat wai nui yi sang |
| I'm allergic to (antibiotics/penicillin). | ngoh dui (kong sang so/poon nei sai lam) gwoh man |

## Emergencies

| Help! | gau meng a! |
|---|---|
| Thief! | cheung ye a! |
| Call the police! | giu ging chaat! |
| Call an ambulance! | giu gau seung che! |
| Watch out! | siu sam! |

*Detail: Man Mo Temple*

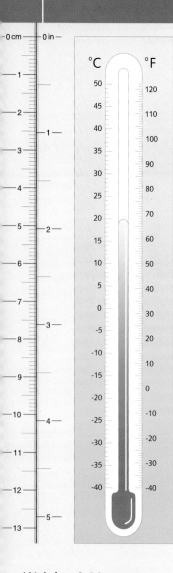

# Conversion Table

## Clothing Sizes

*Measurements approximate only; try before you buy.*

### Women's Clothing

| Aust/NZ | 8 | 10 | 12 | 14 | 16 | 18 |
|---|---|---|---|---|---|---|
| Europe | 36 | 38 | 40 | 42 | 44 | 46 |
| Japan | 5 | 7 | 9 | 11 | 13 | 15 |
| UK | 8 | 10 | 12 | 14 | 16 | 18 |
| USA | 6 | 8 | 10 | 12 | 14 | 16 |

### Women's Shoes

| Aust/NZ | 5 | 6 | 7 | 8 | 9 | 10 |
|---|---|---|---|---|---|---|
| Europe | 35 | 36 | 37 | 38 | 39 | 40 |
| France only | 35 | 36 | 38 | 39 | 40 | 42 |
| Japan | 22 | 23 | 24 | 25 | 26 | 27 |
| UK | 3½ | 4½ | 5½ | 6½ | 7½ | 8½ |
| USA | 5 | 6 | 7 | 8 | 9 | 10 |

### Men's Clothing

| Aust/NZ | 92 | 96 | 100 | 104 | 108 | 112 |
|---|---|---|---|---|---|---|
| Europe | 46 | 48 | 50 | 52 | 54 | 56 |
| Japan | S | | M | M | | L |
| UK | 35 | 36 | 37 | 38 | 39 | 40 |
| USA | 35 | 36 | 37 | 38 | 39 | 40 |

### Men's Shirts (Collar Sizes)

| Aust/NZ | 38 | 39 | 40 | 41 | 42 | 43 |
|---|---|---|---|---|---|---|
| Europe | 38 | 39 | 40 | 41 | 42 | 43 |
| Japan | 38 | 39 | 40 | 41 | 42 | 43 |
| UK | 15 | 15½ | 16 | 16½ | 17 | 17½ |
| USA | 15 | 15½ | 16 | 16½ | 17 | 17½ |

### Men's Shoes

| Aust/NZ | 7 | 8 | 9 | 10 | 11 | 12 |
|---|---|---|---|---|---|---|
| Europe | 41 | 42 | 43 | 44½ | 46 | 47 |
| Japan | 26 | 27 | 27.5 | 28 | 29 | 30 |
| UK | 7 | 8 | 9 | 10 | 11 | 12 |
| USA | 7½ | 8½ | 9½ | 10½ | 11½ | 12½ |

## Weights & Measures

### Weight

1kg = 2.2lb
1lb = 0.45kg
1g = 0.04oz
1oz = 28g

### Volume

1 litre = 0.26 US gallons
1 US gallon = 3.8 litres
1 litre = 0.22 imperial gallons
1 imperial gallon = 4.55 litres

## Length & Distance

1 inch = 2.54cm
1cm = 0.39 inches
1m = 3.3ft = 1.1yds
1ft = 0.3m
1km = 0.62 miles
1 mile = 1.6km

# lonely planet

Lonely Planet is the world's most successful independent travel information company with offices in Australia, the USA, UK and France. With a reputation for comprehensive, reliable travel information, Lonely Planet is a print and electronic publishing leader, with over 650 titles and 22 series catering for travellers' individual needs.

At Lonely Planet we believe that travellers can make a positive contribution to the countries they visit – if they respect their host communities and spend their money wisely. Since 1986 a percentage of the income from books has been donated to aid and human rights projects.

## www.lonelyplanet.com

For news, views and free subscriptions to print and email newsletters, and a full list of LP titles, click on Lonely Planet's award-winning website.

## On the Town

A romantic escape to Paris or a mad shopping dash through New York City, the locals' secret bars or a city's top attractions – whether you have 24hrs to kill or months to explore, Lonely Planet's On the Town products will give you the low-down.

**Condensed guides** are ideal pocket guides for when time is tight. Their quick-view maps, full-colour layout and opinionated reviews help short-term visitors target the top sights and discover the very best eating, shopping and entertainment options a city has to offer.

For more indepth coverage, **City guides** offer insights into a city's character and cultural background as well as providing extensive coverage of where to eat, stay and play. **CitySync**, a digital guide for your handheld unit, allows you to reference stacks of opinionated, well-researched travel information. Portable and durable **City Maps** are perfect for locating those back-street bars or hard-to-find local haunts.

*'Ideal for a generation of fast movers.'*

– *Gourmet Traveller* on Condensed guides

## Condensed Guides

- Amsterdam
- Athens
- Bangkok
- Barcelona
- Beijing (Sept 2003)
- Boston
- Brussels (March 2004)
- Chicago
- Dublin
- Florence (May 2003)
- Frankfurt
- Las Vegas (May 2003)
- Lisbon (Sept 2003)
- London
- Los Angeles
- Madrid
- Milan (March 2004)
- New Orleans
- New York City
- Paris
- Prague
- Rome
- San Francisco
- Singapore
- Sydney
- Tokyo
- Venice
- Washington, DC

# index

*See also separate indexes for Places to Eat (p. 126), Places to Stay (p. 127),
Shops (p. 127) and Sights with map references (p. 128).*

## PLACES TO EAT

## PLACES TO STAY

## SHOPS

51/F Cheung Kong Corter.
2 Queen's Road

# sights – quick index